The

PRODUCTION NOTEBOOKS

The *P*roduction Notebooks

THEATRE IN PROCESS

Volume II

EDITED, WITH AN INTRODUCTION BY

MARK BLY

The First Picture Show at American Conservatory Theater
and Mark Taper Forum
By Corey Madden

Shakespeare Rapid Eye Movement at Bayerisches Staatsschauspiel
By Lise Ann Johnson

In the Blood at The Joseph Papp Public Theater/
New York Shakespeare Festival
By John Dias

Geography at Yale Repertory Theatre
By Katherine Profeta

THEATRE COMMUNICATIONS GROUP
NEW YORK

The Production Notebooks: Theatre in Process, Volume II is published by
Theatre Communications Group, Inc., 355 Lexington Ave., New York, NY 10017-6603.

The First Picture Show notebook by Corey Madden. Production photographs at
Mark Taper Forum copyright © 1999 by Craig Schwartz; production photographs
at ACT copyright © 1999 by Ken Friedman.

Shakespeare Rapid Eye Movement notebook by Lise Ann Johnson. Production photographs
copyright © 1993 by Wilfried Hösl; set design sketches copyright © 1993 by Christian
Schaller; program/magazine cover design copyright © 1993 by Bayerisches
Staatsschauspiel.

In the Blood notebook by John Dias. Production photographs copyright © 1999
by Michal Daniel.

Geography notebook by Katherine Profeta. Production photographs copyright © 1997
by T. Charles Erickson; design sketches copyright © 1997 by Liz Prince.

The Literary Managers and Dramaturgs of the Americas (LMDA) was instrumental
in the promoting and funding of this project.

This publication is made possible in part with public funds from the New York State Council
on the Arts, a State Agency.

TCG books are exclusively distributed to the book trade by Consortium Book Sales and
Distribution, 1045 Westgate Dr., St. Paul, MN 55114.

The Library of Congress has catalogued Volume I as follows:

> The production notebooks / edited and with an introduction by Mark Bly.
> ISBN 1-55936-110-7
> 1. Theater—Production and direction. 2. Dramaturges—United States—Diaries.
> I. Bly, Mark. II. Series.
> PN2053.P75   1996
> 792'.0232—dc20   05—45987
> CIP

Volume II ISBN 1-55936-189-1

Cover photo is Ralph Lemon (standing) and Goulei Tchépoho in the Rock Throwing
scene from the Yale Repertory Theatre production of *Geography*. Copyright © 1997
by T. Charles Erickson.

Book and cover design by Lisa Govan

First Edition, November 2001

✂❦✂❦✂❦✂❦✂❦✂❦✂❦✂❦✂❦✂❦✂❦✂❦

I dedicate this book with love to the memory of my father, Myrle S. Bly, and my uncle, Selmer ("Sam") Bly, two great old Norwegian storytellers who first taught me about the value of communal history.

✂❦✂❦✂❦✂❦✂❦✂❦✂❦✂❦✂❦✂❦✂❦✂❦

CONTENTS

ACKNOWLEDGMENTS

This book would not have been possible without the generosity and cooperation of many people. I am extremely grateful to the artistic directors, stage directors, other artists, technicians and theatre staffs who produced, staged and participated in the work described in this volume. I would especially like to thank Gordon Davidson, Carey Perloff, George Wolfe, Stan Wojewodski, Jr., Victoria Nolan, David Gordon, Ain Gordon, David Esbjornson, Robert Lepage, Ralph Lemon, Ann Rosenthal, Suzan-Lori Parks, Peter Novak, Jan Hartley, Ken Friedman, Craig Schwartz, T. Charles Erickson, Wilfried Hösl, Michal Daniel, Christian Schaller, Liz Prince and Rachel Fain.

    The Production Notebooks Project was born in 1990, when Anne Cattaneo, the newly elected president of Literary Managers and Dramaturgs of the Americas (LMDA), asked me to suggest endeavors that the organization should be backing. I proposed a series of casebooks, dedicated to recording the creative processes of major theatre artists and the evolution of noteworthy productions. Anne and LMDA raised the funds to begin the project, and the organization has continued its support and encouragement through the preparation of Volume II. I would especially like to thank D. D. Kugler and Virginia Coates, the current president and treasurer; and Geoff Proehl and Jayme Koszyn, two past presidents of LMDA, for their dedication and assistance; and Peggy Marks, an LMDA board member, for taking us gently through the legal labyrinths.

    Funding to begin this series was provided by the Andrew W.

Mellon Foundation. Additional funding was provided by the Ettinger Foundation. I am deeply grateful for the opportunity these organizations provided. Rachel Newton Bellow, formerly of the Mellon Foundation, was especially supportive of our aspirations; and I am once again grateful to Rocco Landesman for his prescient backing of this project.

I am indebted to Terence Nemeth and Kathy Sova of Theatre Communications Group for their expertise, perseverance and boundless patience during the preparation of this volume. Kathy provided the personal attention and good will that made my life substantially easier. Ruth Hein was our alert copy editor.

Both Elizabeth Bennett and Merv Antonio were kind enough to give me the benefit of their good advice, assistance and encouragement in the development of this volume and this series. I also want to thank James and Catherine Johnson, who provided assistance at a crucial moment to ensure that our *Shakespeare Rapid Eye Movement* notebook got off to a good start.

I am grateful to my wife, Pamela K. Anderson, who has assisted me at every stage of this project, from the initial proposals and contracts, through the editorial process, to the final drive to pull together all the details of an effort involving multiple authors and several institutions.

Finally, I most especially thank the four dramaturgs who made this volume possible: John Dias, Lise Ann Johnson, Corey Madden and Katherine Profeta. They gave up holidays, weekends and evenings with family and friends to finish these notebooks on time. In the midst of a multitude of other professional obligations, they managed to take the notes and record the moments that would give our readers insight into the sometimes chaotic process of theatre production. I thank them for the excellent job they did and for affirming manyfold the confidence I had in them.

. . . the theatre, strictly speaking, is not a business at all, but a collection of individualized chaos that operates best when it is allowed to flower in its proper medley of disorder, derangement, irregularity and confusion. Its want of method, its untidiness and its discord are not the totality of anarchy it so often seems to be, but the natural progression of its own strange patterns, which sometimes arrange themselves into a wonderful symmetry that is inexplicable to the bewildered outsider.

—MOSS HART

Act One, 1959

The classification of the constituents of a chaos, nothing less is here essayed.

—HERMAN MELVILLE

Moby Dick, 1851

INTRODUCTION

> You should write it down because if you don't write it
> down then they will come along and tell the future that
> we did not exist. You should write it down and you should
> hide it under a rock.
>
> —SUZAN-LORI PARKS
>
> Speech of YES AND GREENS BLACK-EYED PEAS CORNBREAD,
> From *The Death of the Last Black Man in the Whole Entire World*,
> 1992

In the early 1990s, I created the Production Notebooks Project to rectify in some small way the astonishing dearth of documentation of the artistic process in contemporary American theatre. It is rare in the theatre world for even the most imaginatively conceived stagings to be chronicled beyond the typical archival gestures: a promptbook; a grainy videotape secreted away in the bowels of the library at Lincoln Center; and a smattering of hastily written reviews and publicity photographs. The artistic explorations of the preproduction and rehearsal periods are largely forgotten in the frenetic rush to opening night, and only faint traces and shadowy impressions of an artistic journey witnessed by a select few are left behind.

I envisioned a series of notebooks or casebooks, dedicated to recording the creative processes of major theatre artists and the evolution of selected productions. These notebooks would contain, at a minimum, the prerehearsal planning and shaping of the overall vision or approach to the play; the evolution of the staged text, particularly in the development of a new script; and an explo-

ration of the day-to-day rehearsal process. With the encourage-
ment and support of the not-for-profit professional organization,
Literary Managers and Dramaturgs of the Americas (LMDA), *The
Production Notebooks* series was born.

Volume I included the work of the late director Garland
Wright and dramaturg Jim Lewis, on "The Clytemnestra Project" at
the Guthrie Theater; director Robert Wilson and dramaturg Chris
Baker, on *Danton's Death* at the Alley Theatre; poet Ntozake Shange,
director Talvin Wilks and dramaturg Shelby Jiggetts on *The Love
Space Demands* at Crossroads Theatre Company; and director Domi-
nique Serrand and dramaturg Paul Walsh on the company-created
Children of Paradise: Shooting a Dream at Theatre de la Jeune Lune.

The primary criterion for inclusion in the series has been
that the individuals collaborating on the production must be artists
of consequence who have a history of creating imaginative, thought-
provoking work.

A second requirement is the availability of an analytical
writer, versed in all aspects of theatre, who would be intimately
involved in the work from conception through closing. As I indi-
cated in Volume I, at most not-for-profit resident theatres in the
United States today, there are artists, known as "dramaturgs," who
meet these criteria.

A final key requisite is that both the producing theatre and
the stage director are willing to allow the dramaturg's observations
of private meetings and rehearsals to be published.

Critical approbation has not been a factor in the selection of
productions included in either the first or the second volume. The
stagework of these artists merits chronicling, whether the final production is acclaimed a failure or a success. The evolution of each
project is what interests me the most, especially commentary on
the obstacles encountered by the artists, and the temporary aesthetic detours and artistic choices made.

A residual effect of these notebooks will be the promotion

of a greater awareness of the creative work being done by dramaturgs in resident theatres today. While there is no "single origin theory" of dramaturgy in the United States, significant pioneering work in the emerging field of production dramaturgy occurred in the 1980s, at theatres such as the Eureka Theatre Company, the Guthrie Theater and South Coast Repertory, to name a few.

Prior to this time, dramaturgs traditionally had been office-bound researchers, script readers and text editors. But in the 1980s at theatres such as these, dramaturgs began to take on a more collaborative role, participating actively in the rehearsal process. These artists, often called "production dramaturgs," to reflect the precise nature of their work, can function in a multifaceted manner, helping the director and other artists to interpret and shape the sociological, textual, acting, directing and design values, as well as culturally sensitive aesthetic approaches.

In addition to growth within the field, several dramaturgs have chosen to become artistic directors of major theatre organizations, a logical result of the dramaturg's wide-ranging, yet in-depth, knowledge of dramatic literature and the theatrical process. A few enterprising dramaturgs have also ventured into opera, dance, film and television, extending the profession into other disciplines. The *Geography* notebook, by Katherine Profeta, in this volume, is an example of this extension of the profession into the field of dance. Also, many dramaturgs maintain dual careers, such as dramaturg/playwright or dramaturg/critic. To borrow a phrase from the paleontologist Stephen Jay Gould, dramaturgs in the United States and Canada are continuing to evolve, transform and "bristle with multiple possibilities."

The four production notebooks contained in this book have all been created by practicing dramaturgs: Corey Madden, associate artistic director of the Mark Taper Forum, on *The First Picture Show*, written by David Gordon and Ain Gordon, directed by David Gordon, and coproduced by the Mark Taper Forum and the American Conservatory Theater (1999); John Dias, now associate producer at The Joseph Papp Public Theater/New York Shakespeare Festival, on *In the Blood*, by Suzan-Lori Parks, directed by David Esbjornson (1999); Katherine Profeta, then a student dramaturg at the Yale Repertory Theatre, on *Geography*, conceived and directed by Ralph Lemon (1997); and Lise Ann Johnson, freelance dramaturg, on *Shakespeare Rapid Eye Movement*, directed by Robert Lepage for the Bayerisches Staatsschauspiel in Munich, Germany (1993).

Although the production notebooks in this volume were not commissioned as models for the practice of production dramaturgy, the notebooks do reflect some of the professional challenges and opportunities of a dramaturg's daily life in the theatre. In three of the four stagings documented in this volume, the chronicler is also the production's official dramaturg. In the fourth instance, Robert Lepage's *Shakespeare Rapid Eye Movement* in Munich, the freelance dramaturg, Lise Ann Johnson, documented the staging for this volume, although her formal role was as observer and not dramaturg.

I selected these particular productions for several key reasons. David and Ain Gordon's work with the Pick Up Company has consistently challenged the existing vocabularies of stage presentation and performance techniques. My interest was heightened when I discovered that an early impetus for *The First Picture Show* was the connection David Gordon made between his own largely undocumented stagework and the work done by many silent film pioneers whose films have all but disappeared. One song in *The First Picture Show*, delivered by the filmmaker Billy, states the problem plaintively:

No film I made exists
Only titles, only lists,
Only year and cast and cost,
The films themselves have all been lost.
They're only in my head.
And when I'm dead,

And all is said and done,
There isn't even one for anyone to see
The joke's on me
No one will ever see
The pictures that I made.

As is clear from these lyrics, David Gordon and Ain Gordon's concern for preserving evidence of artistic achievement is in accord with my original impulse for the creation of the series.

While only in her thirties, Suzan-Lori Parks is already recognized as a major voice in the American theatre, and one whose process as a playwright deserves to be chronicled, particularly in relation to her stylistic explorations and questioning of traditional historical perspectives. *In the Blood* is in part inspired by Nathaniel Hawthorne's classic, *The Scarlet Letter*, and offers up a provocative stage portrait of a bewildered Hester of the Streets in a contemporary American urban setting.

Ralph Lemon's multidisciplinary project, *Geography*, produced at the Yale Repertory Theatre, brings together an extensive group of collaborators, including dancers, percussionists, designers, a poet, two composers and an installation artist, from places as diverse as Côte d' Ivoire, Guinea, Spain and the United States, to create a work for the theatre. Many of Lemon's collaborators had no previous resident theatre experience. The fusion of cultures and perspectives generated a unique working process rarely encountered in the theatre world.

Finally, when I learned in 1992 that the internationally renowned French-Canadian director Robert Lepage was creating a project that linked the geography of dreams, the works of Shakespeare and the collective unconscious, I was immediately drawn to what came to be known as *Shakespeare Rapid Eye Movement*. Staged at the Bayerisches Staatsschauspiel in Munich, Germany, using the resident acting company, the piece presented three "dream" excerpts in German translation from Shakespeare's *Richard III, A Midsummer Night's Dream* and *The Tempest*. As the reader will discover, cross-cultural currents influenced the resulting production in unexpected ways.

At their best, the production notebooks in this volume reflect a desire on the part of the artists involved to stretch the boundaries of theatrical expression and to challenge existing collaborative models that are often comforting but calcified. Robert Lepage, in a 1994 interview with Karen Fricker, observed about his creative process:

> There is no recipe, no series of rules, no theory behind what we do. You cannot put a Shakespeare play and a Tennessee Williams play in the same microwave oven and expect them to be "done." How is this meal going to be cooked? We'll have to discover that as we go along.

The four notebooks that follow confirm that there are no "recipes" for achieving a successful artistic collaboration. But the notebooks do record the artistic journeys made and the problems encountered and the temporary detours taken. Ultimately, it is my desire that the notebooks will have a long-term impact on theatre as we enter the twenty-first century, offering rare windows into the creative lives of some of our leading theatre artists, and perhaps in doing so, awakening future artists to unexpected acts of the imagination.

Mark Bly
Project Director and Editor

Mark Bly is Associate Artistic Director of the Yale Repertory Theatre and Chair of the Playwriting Department at the Yale School of Drama. His varied professional experience includes dramaturging more than sixty productions at theatres such as Arena Stage, Washington, D.C.; the Guthrie Theater, Minneapolis; Seattle Repertory Theatre, Seattle; Long Wharf Theatre, New Haven, CT; and Yale Repertory Theatre, New Haven, CT.

The FIRST PICTURE SHOW

AT AMERICAN CONSERVATORY THEATER

AND MARK TAPER FORUM

by Corey Madden

The First Picture Show began in 1995 when the Mark Taper Forum commissioned David and Ain Gordon to create a work of theatre, dance and music for its stage. In 1998 the American Conservatory Theater (ACT) joined the project as a development partner, and the show premiered on the ACT stage in San Francisco in May 1999. The production debuted on the Taper stage in Los Angeles in August 1999. Directed by David Gordon, *The First Picture Show* moves seamlessly from drama to dance, dialogue to song, present to past. It changes rapidly from one performance style to another, one story to another, one character to another, to create a constantly shifting, fast-paced and complex new amalgam. Corey Madden, who is the associate artistic director at the Mark Taper Forum, served as the production's dramaturg through its four years, three readings, four workshops and two major productions.

At American Conservatory Theater

BOOK AND LYRICS BY	Ain Gordon, David Gordon
MUSIC BY	Jeanine Tesori
DIRECTED AND CHOREOGRAPHED BY	David Gordon
ASSOCIATE DIRECTOR	Ain Gordon
SCENERY BY	Robert Brill
COSTUMES BY	Judith Anne Dolan
LIGHTING BY	Jennifer Tipton
SOUND BY	Garth Hemphill

MUSICAL DIRECTOR/PERFORMER	Peter Maleitzke
PROJECTION DESIGN BY	Jan Hartley
DRAMATURG	Corey Madden
CASTING BY	Meryl Lind Shaw;
	Stanley Soble, C.S.A.;
	James Calleri
HAIR AND MAKEUP BY	Rick Echols
ASSISTANT TO THE DIRECTORS	Karen Graham
ASSOCIATE MUSICAL DIRECTOR/	
PIANIST	Julie Homi
STAGE MANAGER	Ray Gin
PRODUCTION ADVISOR	Ed Fitzgerald

CAST

HENRY HOOKS, CARL LAEMMLE, CHAIRMAN HOWE, CLEO MADISON, MAC	John Apicella
ANNE FIRST (AGE 99)	Anne Gee Byrd
CAMERAWOMAN, ATTENDANT	Cindy Cheung
THELMA MARCH, LOIS WEBER	Kathleen Conry
CONNIE GARDNER, GENE GAUNTIER, MAY FURSTMANN, W. STEVEN BUSH	Norma Fire
BILLY'S ASSISTANT, ATTENDANT, NELL SHIPMAN	Karen Graham
ANNE FIRST (AGES 15–38)	Ellen Greene
JANE FURSTMANN	Dinah Lenney
BILLY FRIEND, STORAGE MAN, JUSTICE MCKENNA, IDA MAY PARK, DUDLEY M. HUGHES	Ken Marks
LOUIS FURSTMANN, MARGERY WILSON, SECRETARY SLICKLEN, MONTY LATOUR, MASS	Evan Pappas

NURSE TINA, CINDY SU, MARION E. WONG, T.V. NEWSCASTER	Jeanne Sakata
REV. WILBUR F. CRAFTS, ALICE GUY BLACHÉ, MRS. KLINKMAN, MOVIE ASSISTANT, AWARDS HOST	Valda Setterfield
ATTENDANT, CUSTOMS OFFICIAL, NEWSMAN	Michael Gene Sullivan
THE DOCTOR, PERCY WATERS, BEN TYLER	Harry Waters, Jr.

At Mark Taper Forum

BOOK AND LYRICS BY	Ain Gordon, David Gordon
MUSIC BY	Jeanine Tesori
DIRECTED AND CHOREOGRAPHED BY	David Gordon
ASSOCIATE DIRECTOR	Ain Gordon
SET DESIGNED BY	Robert Brill
COSTUMES DESIGNED BY	Judith Dolan
LIGHTING DESIGNED BY	Jennifer Tipton
SOUND DESIGNED BY	Jon Gottlieb and Philip G. Allen
MUSIC DIRECTOR	Kimberly Grigsby
DRAMATURG	Corey Madden
CASTING	Stanley Soble, C.S.A.; Meryl Lind Shaw; James Calleri, C.S.A.; Vince Liebhart
PRODUCTION STAGE MANAGER	Ed Fitzgerald
STAGE MANAGER	Lisa J. Snodgrass
ASSISTANT TO THE DIRECTORS	Karen Graham

CAST

ANNE FIRST (AGE 99)	Estelle Parsons
CENSOR, CUSTOMS OFFICIAL, TRAIN ANNOUNCER, MOVIE CREW, SECOND PIANIST	Christian Nova
LOUIE'S MOTHER, LOUIE'S FRIEND, MOVIE CREW, NEWSMAN	Chuck Rosen
LOIS WEBER, THELMA MARCH	Kathleen Conry
ANNE FIRST (AGES 15–38), JANE FURSTMANN	Ellen Greene
MAY FURSTMANN, CONNIE GARDNER, GENE GAUNTIER	Norma Fire
CENSOR, PERCY WATERS, MOVIE CREW, CLEO MADISON, REP. HUGHES	Harry Waters, Jr.
LOUIS FURSTMANN, HENRY HOOKS, MONTY LATOUR, MARGERY WILSON	Steven Skybell
NURSE TINA, CINDY SU, JUSTICE MCKENNA, MARION E. WONG	Jeanne Sakata
LOUIE'S FRIEND, JANE'S ASSISTANT, BILLY'S ASSISTANT, NELL SHIPMAN	Karen Graham
CARL LAEMMLE, AD-MAN, BILLY FRIEND, IDA MAY PARK, SECOND PIANIST	Ken Marks
REV. WILBUR E. CRAFTS, ALICE GUY BLACHÉ, MOVIE CREW, AWARDS HOST	Valda Setterfield
T.V. NEWSCASTER, MOVIE CREW	Kerry K. Carnahan
NAOMI THE PIANO PLAYER	Kimberly Grigsby
ANNE FIRST (AGE 99), PERFORMANCES SEPTEMBER 7–12	Anne Gee Byrd

The First Picture Show concerns the past and present of Anne First, a silent film director who made her last film in 1932 at the age of thirty-eight. Confined to a retirement home for members of the motion-picture industry, she is surrounded by many of her former colleagues. At ninety-nine, Anne is unhappy and isolated from everyone in the home. She is haunted by her memories of being a young filmmaker and by some unnamed betrayal in her past. By chance Anne's great-great-niece, Jane, discovers her long-lost connection to Anne through a diary someone sent her. Jane decides to make a documentary about Anne's life. When they first meet, Anne refuses to talk to Jane, so Jane decides to make her film about the residents in the home, instead.

Memory sequences reveal Anne's life from her girlhood days in Ohio through her last filmmaking experience. We see her early success in silent films, when opportunities are widely available, and later her furious struggle to continue making films against the almost insurmountable obstacles of censorship, consolidation of the studios and changing tastes.

In Act I the audience sees Anne leave home and become a successful young director of silent films. The first act also chronicles Anne and Jane's first encounter as well as Jane's filming of the residents. In addition it follows the fortunes of Anne's brother, Louis, as he tries to become a movie mogul and decides to move to Los Angeles. Interspersed with these stories are a number of songs and scenes about the fight to control the content of film through censorship. Prime mover in this story line is a character named Reverend Crafts.

The second act begins with a pastiche of early women film-makers who sing an anthem about how they made history. Jane continues to work on her film by interviewing Percy, an African-American who pioneered race films, and Tina, the granddaughter of an Asian-American actress and assistant director. Anne grudgingly admits that her niece is getting good material. In the memory sequences we follow the fortunes of Anne and Louis, who come to a grave impasse when Louis asks for Anne's help in establishing a studio.

In Act II censorship begins to have an impact on Anne. Eventually she is called to Washington to testify against government censorship. There she runs into her estranged brother, Louis. In his testimony he is trapped by Reverend Crafts into admitting that his own sister's films are immoral. This is the final blow for their tenuous relationship. Returning to Hollywood, Anne is forced to face both increasing restrictions on the content of her films and loss of support from the studios. She makes a final film, *A Sister's Journey,* using her own money. When it fails, critically and financially, she leaves the business.

Through the diary Jane pieces together Anne's failure and her estrangement from Louis. Jane reveals Louis's eulogy to Anne, which causes Anne to come to terms with her losses. Jane also discovers three reels of *A Sister's Journey* back in Ohio. Both of these discoveries help Anne admit what is causing her so much pain. Jane finishes her movie and receives an award. The last moment of the play is a taped interview of Anne, filmed just before her death at 100, in which she speaks about the legacy of being a pathfinder in the early days of film.

INTRODUCTION

When I first met David Gordon in the spring of 1992, he was just beginning to explore the possibilities of working in the theatre as a writer/director after more than twenty years as a postmodern choreographer. He was coming to the University of California, Los Angeles (UCLA), in the fall to teach and to develop a new theatre work called *Punch and Judy Get a Divorce,* and he hoped that the Mark Taper Forum would cosponsor the residency and provide some theatrical advice. I had worked on a number of collaborative projects with UCLA, including a joint presentation of Robert Lepage's *A Dragon's Trilogy* the previous year, so I was tapped by the Taper to develop support from various sources on campus and to offer casting advice and producing support over David Gordon's month-long workshop. Once involved with David and his work, I became captivated by his approach to making theatre and have remained so for many years.

Although David's dance work had always contained text, at UCLA David began to be interested in the structure and intentions of dramatic writing. After I had the opportunity to read one of his man-uscripts, it seemed to me that what was unique about David's work was the connection between his physical compositions and his writ-ing. His prose had many of the same characteristics as his dance: a focus on ordinary human behavior, fast-paced rhythm and repetition.

In 1995 the Taper commissioned David Gordon and his son, Ain Gordon, to create a work of dance, theatre and music that eventually became *The First Picture Show.* In the spring of 1998 we were joined by a development partner, American Conservatory Theater (ACT), who coproduced the world premiere of the work in May 1999 in San Francisco. It debuted at the Mark Taper Forum in August 1999. Along the way the project went through four workshops and three readings in addition to the two productions.

The first impulses for the play came from David Gordon and Ain Gordon's interest in silent films and their desire to make a work specifically for the Taper and its audiences. During the research phase a chance encounter with Anthony Slide's *Early Women Directors* pointed them in the direction of unknown women directors of the silent film era. They created a fictional composite of early film directors and named the character Anne First.

The First Picture Show attempts to create a world where past and present are alive in the minds and bodies of the company. The most central of its themes have to do with artists and art making, with independence and obligation, with love and death. In construction it is a piece that draws on conventions from theatre, film, dance and musical theatre.

The process of working on *The First Picture Show* (which was also called *Silent Movie* and *Who's Anne First?* in previous drafts) can be broken up into four periods: research and creation of the text; workshopping of the text alone; workshopping of the music and text; and production. My role as dramaturg was naturally different in each phase and intensified as we moved toward production. Much of my work focused on the structural and thematic challenges created by a script with numerous characters, story lines and theatrical styles. My goal was to assist the artists in blending postmodern performance techniques, dramatic structure and musical theatre conventions into a unique new amalgam.

The great challenge for me as a dramaturg was to see clearly what the other artists aimed to achieve—structurally, tonally, philosophically—and to help them realize it through analysis of the text. Over the three years my analysis took every form imaginable, including rafts of notes, lists of questions, scene breakdowns, storyboarding and many, many discussions about the day's work. In sifting through the notebooks I've kept, I'm reminded that an ambitious work of theatre takes a significant time to come into focus, though its essence is often established early on.

Estelle Parsons as Anne First (age 99) in the Mark Taper Forum production.
Photograph by Craig Schwartz.

December 1995

We have just finished presenting *The Family Business* on the mainstage at the Taper. This is the Obie Award-winning dance-theatre piece that David Gordon and Ain Gordon and Valda Setterfield made last year in New York for Dance Theatre Workshop. David and Valda are husband and wife, and Ain is their son. Presenting the work of these artists has been satisfying, but working on a new piece with David and Ain is what we really want to do next.

Ain and David and I meet with Gordon Davidson (artistic director of Center Theatre Group/Mark Taper Forum) to officially commission them to create a new piece for the Taper. They are calling the project *Silent Movie*. It will be a work of theatre with music, movement, singing and film.

David and Ain have both done a lot of reading about the early days of Hollywood. David is very interested in the silent-film technique of communicating meaning through gesture. Ain is concerned with the issue of censorship in Hollywood. We will support the commission with a developmental workshop once the first draft comes in.

Summer 1996

The Pick Up Company is invited to be in residence at Jacob's Pillow, an important dance festival. David Gordon founded the Pick Up Company in 1978 to provide a stable yet fluid structure for the presentation of his work. In 1994 the mission of the company expanded to include the work of Ain Gordon. Although the number of artists involved varies from project to project, there is a core group that continues to be involved in the development and performance of new work.

The residency at Jacob's Pillow will allow David several weeks to explore the physical vocabulary of silent film and compose sections of the choreography. The workshop performance will also give David and Ain their first chance to see how the piece connects with an audience. In this workshop David will work with professional dancers rather than actors. This will allow him to improvise and revise the choreography, a key ingredient in the early part of his process. David and Ain will write in the evenings while they are there.

I would like to see the workshop in July, but I am too far along in my pregnancy to travel. The report from David is very positive, and plans are made for a reading of the script some time in the fall. David and Ain (with Valda) will rent a house in Montauk, New York, in August and they plan to finish a draft there.

October 1996

The script arrives with a new title: *Who's Anne First?* David and Ain have come to Los Angeles for a reading of the script for Gordon Davidson and the rest of the artistic staff. Since my son, Ezra, was born in September, I am on maternity leave. Kindly, David and Ain came to the house for our first real dramaturgical conversation.

The script is a difficult read. It is not formatted like a traditional text. There are no scene breaks, and it's confusing how the doubling works. "Songs" are marked in capital letters but not in any other way.

As we go along through the script, I learn that this format reflects how they see the work for the stage. David explains more precisely the theatrical conventions of the event, how characters will double, the stylistic shifts and the constantly choreographed actions. Songs come right out of dialogue and disappear right back into dialogue.

Like *The Family Business,* this piece will be in a state of perpetual transition, shifting rapidly from one character to another, from one style to another, from one story to another. As in *Wally's Ghost* (by Ain Gordon), it's clear from the outset that each story line is meant to inform another, and the story lines may substitute for one another. In classic Gordon fashion, it's funny and angry and urgent in tone. The characters are feisty, independent, working class and mostly Jewish.

After they leave, I read the play again, out loud. It's exciting but seems incredibly complex. I worry about it being diffuse. I think this, perversely enough, is exactly what they intend the piece to be.

The play primarily follows the story of Anne First, treating her life both in the present in a nursing home for "old movie folks" and in the past, from orphan in Ohio at age six to silent film director in Los Angeles at age thirty-eight.

In the present the play includes the story of Anne's great-great niece, Jane, a struggling "30-something," who is on contract to make a CD-ROM about the silent-film era. Jane wants to interview her aunt, but Anne refuses to talk about the past, even though it haunts her in the form of memories and a ghost. The story in the present also concerns the denizens (Henry Hooks, Connie Gardener, Thelma March, Percy Waters, Nurse, Doctor) of the "old movie folks" home and their stories from the past, which Jane records. Jane's live-in lover, Ben, also figures in the present as a goad and a supporter.

The part of the play concerning the past takes up far more stage time and is quite complex. Some story lines intersect. Others have an implied impact. Some are narrative in nature. Others are presented as vaudevilles of historical fact. The seven subplots in the story from the past are tied together for the most part through Anne:

- ✳ Anne's life as a filmmaker, her early joy and her later failures
- ✳ Anne and Naomi, a friendship that sours as Anne becomes more invested in films
- ✳ Anne and Louis, a relationship that is destroyed when, in order to be free from family and obligation, Anne rejects his offer to go into business
- ✳ Louis and May, a loving couple who become rich as film presenters in Ohio
- ✳ Slicklen, Klinkman and Howe, a vaudeville of citizens as censors
- ✳ Reverend Crafts, a melodrama about the manipulative efforts of religious leaders to control artists as a way to gain political control
- ✳ Carl Laemmle and Lois Weber, a vaudeville about freedom of content threatened by censorship and the marketplace

All of this is intended to be set to music!

I don't know what the doubling will be, but we talked about the cast numbering ten to fifteen when we first commissioned the piece. David has said that in his casting he wants to play with age, gender and race, as he did in *The Family Business* and *Punch and Judy Get a Divorce*. Male and female company members will each play both genders and a broad range of ages.

I'm worried about the number of story lines. I just don't see how an audience can connect to that many. Of the themes, I am least compelled by censorship, especially the climax at the congressional hearings. It doesn't seem to connect to the rest of the play except in the hearings. On the other hand, thematically, it may be the richest aspect of the play. I know that David and Ain are passionate about it.

We send David and Ain away with the promise of a four-week workshop later this season.

In my last conversation with David and Ain before they leave, I broach the subject of the number of story lines. David bristles a bit, as he is likely to do when you give him advice that has a "traditionalist" bent. "Why can't I have this many story lines? Look at screenplays. They do."

I make a chart that shows how each story line flows in the script and, page by page, where we are in the storytelling. This turns out to be a very effective tool that quantifies how stage time is being used. It gives Ain and David an objective way to evaluate their priorities.

Winter 1996–97: Reading in New York

I attend the reading of *Who's Anne First?* in New York. Sponsored by the Pick Up Company, this reading is intended to give potential Pick Up sponsors, and other folks who might underwrite the production, a chance to see the work in progress. Along with such Pick Up Company "regulars" as Lola Pashalinski, David and Ain perform roles in the reading, conveying a sense of the way nontraditional casting will inform the aesthetic of the piece.

David and Ain create events in which one is always aware of performance. They dispense with the traditional theatrical fantasy of verisimilitude and instead encourage a more imaginative interaction between audience and performer. When David played Auntie Annie, in *The Family Business,* wearing his black combat pants, black T-shirt and a yoke apron, he communicated a subversiveness he is intent on having in this piece as well. He wants the audience to play along with him, to see the event as casual, "made up," spontaneous. Its artifice is obvious, humorous and accessible. Stripped of illusion, untethered to gender, race or age, his performers reveal the human body and soul, the character and the actor joined. It is David's belief that art communicates more deeply when the audience is aware and actively participates in the creation of performance.

One of the facts of this project is that it has two writers, David and Ain, with different experiences and different aesthetic ideas. This is their second major collaboration as writers, so they have a way of working and a shared set of interests as writers. Their process involves writing at the computer in David's loft. Sometimes one or the other will bring material to a work session, but most often they write together, even trading off on the typing. Once they have a draft of a scene finished, they read the material out loud, each playing his designated characters.

In their collaborative artistic statement, written when they began this project, they declare:

> The chemistry of partner, who does what to/for whom is mysterious. In the relationship of son to father, of father to son, who does what to/for whom is debatable. We work together. We have the benefit of knowing each other but not being the same. We examine, write and edit from compatible but different viewpoints. . . . We are interested in role-playing and reversal, cultural roles and stereotypes, and the reframing of conventional actions under unlikely circumstances. We are interested in how fast today becomes history, [how] history gets distorted and lost. . . . We are interested in dancing that talks and talking that dances and who's walking what fine line and how?

While this piece is very different in ambition from *The Family Business,* the characters of Auntie Annie and Paul in that piece could be prototypes for Anne and Jane in this piece. Not surprisingly David is strongly attached to the concerns of Anne; Ain to those of Jane. The characters seem to evoke the personal tone of each man, as well.

Given this dynamic, it's not surprising that the piece has two

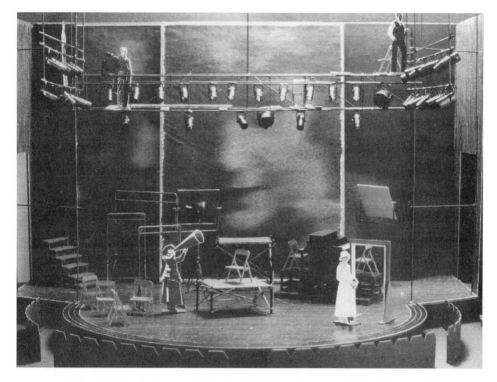

Robert Brill's revised set model for the Mark Taper Forum production. Photograph by Craig Schwartz.

strong characters who appear to be vying for the central position in the play. Quite a few of our discussions are about the relative importance of Anne and Jane. Which one is primary? Are they equally important in the structure of the piece?

March 1997: Developmental workshop without music

The Taper sponsors a four-week workshop in Los Angeles. The goals of this workshop are to get a sense of the piece on its feet as well as assess the current draft. I'm in rehearsal every day for a couple of hours and take time to meet with the team most evenings at the end of rehearsal. I take notes whenever I'm in the room, and I share what I see with Ain and David daily.

In my notes this event is called the foam-core workshop because foam-core board, felt tip pens, duct tape and ingenuity are the ingredients of the visual style that David and Ain create here. The inventions of the foam-core workshop inform all design decisions for the next two years. With these items, David, Ain and Ed Fitzgerald, the stage manager, have constructed amazing props: two cameras, a forced-perspective table top, swinging doors and a television set, as well as a host of silent-movie-style signs and frames. Other elements in the room include folding metal chairs, rolling doors-in-frames and coat racks.

As with *The Family Business* and the workshop of *Punch and Judy Get a Divorce*, David works with very simple elements that can be moved easily by the actors, and that can transform instantly. Transitions into each scene involve the actors' rolling or carrying doors, chairs, signs, and so on. These items are used over and over in the play, so as to create a literal connection, handed as they are from one generation of Anne First's family to another.

David often creates a silly tone with improbable props. The visual for the meeting of the censors is created when four actors rush on with a flat forced-perspective foam-core table, which they hold throughout the scene. The image is laughable and elevates the comic tone of the occasion.

The actors are asked to use the same kind of quick wit in their physical and acting work. One moment they may be asked to create the impression of being in a silent movie. They improvise while a foam-core backdrop moves behind them. Another time the actors might be required to portray the spontaneous and chaotic interactions of a nursing-home recreation room being recorded by a novice filmmaker. The shifts in tone are instantaneous and varied. The effect is like quicksilver, dazzling and mysterious.

In the first days of the workshop David introduces the company to the fundamentals of his "pedestrian" choreography. Often working with groups or pairs, David constructs "walking" dances, built from everyday human movement. With such simple direc-tions as, "I want you to come in the door, walk across the space and sit down in the chair," David builds patterns of movement using more than one actor performing the same or similar business. The contrasts between their bodies moving through space, their rates of entering, walking and sitting form the content of the sequence.

While David spends most of his time on his feet, Ain is watch-ing. In the room, just as David begins to work, he and Ain will dis-cuss how the section will look. David then begins the detailed process of rehearsing company members. Ain functions as a crucial eye to the staging process and as an important guide in the scene work. Every time David finishes a section he takes comments from Ain.

The dialogue between the two continues after rehearsal, at dinner, breakfast, in the car and during work sessions. The carry-over from the rehearsal hall to home is a regular occurrence in the Family Gordon. For David family is integral to his work. David's wife, Valda, has danced and acted in his pieces for thirty years. Ain, their only child, has been an integral part of David and Valda's work since his birth. While all three artists do work independently of one another, their work together is especially important to them.

Ain's familiarity with David's aesthetic interests and concerns is intimate and vast. For the last four years, as a formal collabora-tor and associate director of the Pick Up Company, Ain's creative role has become codified. The two artists work in a manner that takes advantage of their symbiotic relationship, but that also defines a role for each to play. The degree of interconnection has its strengths and its points of friction. Both are seasoned at knowing when a break from constant contact will help the work move forward.

✳

After blocking a large section of the show, David and Ain are edit-ing and moving sections around. I am seeing how David's circular, seamless staging often provides a context that you can't find in the script. His intricate staging of actors moving through space and time creates a constantly shifting point of view.

So far the most beautiful moment of staging has been the sequence introducing Anne's first movie-making, which then transitions into the present in the old folks' home. David has staged a wild and fast-paced filmmaking sequence with the entire ensemble. Some are the actors in the film. Others are grips or assistants. Every one of the fourteen actors is involved in the constantly changing work of filming while Anne-as-a-young-woman directs. Eventually the older Anne takes over the filming, and the scene reverts to memory. The actors circle the stage, gradually shifting their activity from participating in the filmmaking as young people to becoming the ancient ones shuffling into the nursing home, using the folding chairs as walkers. The rush of time is captured. Lives are spent in a matter of moments. The change in perspective is awesome, as is the shift from drama to dance.

Another remarkable aspect of this workshop is that the actors are "singing" without a composer. David has asked the actors to musicalize the song lyrics in rehearsal. Folks are very willing to improvise tunes and to find ways of singing and talking through sections of the material. In some cases actors have invented songs based on their material. Gregory Wallace has made a blues lament out of the Percy Waters monologue. In other cases actors have found a style that will inform the work. John Apicella and Valda Setterfield have made a vaudeville patter number of the censorship scenes. David wants the piece to have the same kind of seamless transitions from scenes to music as there is from drama to dance. While no one expects the "tunes" to survive, this part of the workshop has given him a chance to invent the strategies that will guide the work with a composer.

✳

The workshop showing goes very well, although the script will need trimming. The Taper staff is very enthusiastic, particularly some hard-core folks from marketing, who know what sells and what doesn't. Gordon Davidson and Robert Egan, Taper producing director, and other artistic staffers seem genuinely pleased, although I've had some of my concerns about the show echoed back to me at the coffee and nosh table.

I am concerned about Jane, who seems like a device, not a character. David maintains that Anne is really the main character here. What's off balance is that Jane features heavily in the piece. Ain has a different take on Jane and wants her to be more fully dramatized. Ain and David agree that they need to establish a common goal about her as a character.

My follow-up notes suggest ways of editing that will address the number of story lines and the length of the piece. Using a French scene chart and a marked script, I talk about film editing as a model for how to make a more rapid and intense scene structure for the piece that will allow more stories to share the stage.

Summer 1997

Over the summer David and Ain spend a month in Montauk working on the script together. They rename the piece *The First Picture Show: A Silent Movie-Dance-Comedy-Drama-Musical-History.*

My concern now is introducing David and Ain to composers. It is a major priority to find a composer available and interested in collaborating actively with David and Ain during the writing process and throughout rehearsals. Ain and David have expressed their desire to meet primarily with female composers.

I compile a list of candidates and have my assistant track down CDs and recommendations. Over the phone from Montauk, Ain mentions that there is a lot of buzz about Jeanine Tesori, whose piece, *Violet,* was just produced at New York's Playwrights Horizons. Her name goes on the list.

Fall 1997

The Pick Up Company sponsors its own four-week workshop of *The First Picture Show* at St. Clements Church in New York City. I manage to attend the last two days of rehearsal and the showings. Gordon Davidson plans to come to a showing as well.

The workshop is most effective at conveying how the play will eventually look and feel. David and Ain have repeated the foam-core approach to the scenery. All the rolling stock stays onstage throughout the presentation and constitutes the scenic element of the show. Jennifer Tipton has designed the lights for the evening. The room at St. Clements is bare and black. Jennifer's lights pierce through that darkness to pick up the actors as they move into a scene.

The company wears an array of coats, hats and vaguely "period" suits and dresses. It looks offhand. Of course this is intentional. The actors stay onstage throughout the show, but when they are not in a scene, they are upstage, concealed by darkness. This way one becomes aware of them, but not distracted by them.

The show begins with a wonderful sequence of actor introductions. In pairs, carrying poster-board frames and cards with their own names printed on them, the actors "dance" onstage to introduce themselves. It is a great beginning, reminiscent of the way silent films did their opening credits. This is a funny and witty moment that conveys much about the evening. The signs continue throughout the show at the top of scenes to announce changes of place and time.

By now Jeanine Tesori is David and Ain's first choice for composer. It took some time for the three to meet, since Jeanine delivered her first child, Sienna, six weeks ago, but they are very enthusiastic about her manner of talking about the work process.

Jeanine comes to the showing. Afterward we have a brief moment to talk. She is very enthusiastic about what she saw, even the improvised songs, which she describes as very brave and rather remarkable. I assure her that I'll do everything I can to move things along as soon as she meets with David and Ain. Within a day they have agreed to work together.

Carey Perloff, artistic director of San Francisco's American Conservatory Theater (ACT), attends the workshop and is very excited about the piece. David calls to say that she would like to coproduce it next season.

December 1997

We are on deadline to set the events for the Taper's 1998–99 season, so Gordon Davidson is pressing to hear some music. Jeanine has graciously agreed to produce three songs to show in New York to Gordon, Charles Dillingham (the managing director of the Taper) and me.

Even as they rush to get songs written, I hear from David and Ain that they are thrilled with Jeanine, her work and her personality. Like Ain and David, Jeanine wants to push the form of music-theatre. Their working styles have blended easily, with Jeanine working at the piano with them by her side, scribbling down ideas and cracking jokes.

We all meet in a little space in one of those classic old towers in Times Square. Jeanine has hired three singers and rehearsed them for a day. In the short meeting afterward Gordon agrees to produce the project next season. David, Ain and Jeanine are eager to get to work, so a music workshop is scheduled for March, just three months away.

January 23, 1998

In response to the workshop version of the script, I send a set of notes to David, Ain and now Jeanine, questioning a fundamental notion of the play, multiple story lines. "Having worked with the piece for the last two years, I believe you are on the brink of creating an amazing piece of theatre, but by using stage time to push along five stories, you limit the depth to which you can explore any one of those. After reviewing this draft I feel, in effect, you have too much good material."

I suggest three approaches:

* economize on all exposition and get to the crisis of each scene
* eliminate one or more story lines to make room for more development of the others
* use one character/story line to clarify the nature of the pastiche; for instance, use Jane as a narrator, give her an omniscient point of view

Ken Marks (behind camera); Steven Skybell (with paper); Norma Fire (behind table); Estelle Parsons (in wheelchair); Jeanne Sakata, Chuck Rosen and Kathleen Conry (behind Estelle Parsons). Photograph by Craig Schwartz.

"What's exciting in this draft is that I see a more fluidly structured theatre event, and I think you have already begun the process of economizing.

"About the songs: I loved the work that I heard in New York and see some very good new lyrics in this draft. My questions stem from my concerns about priorities: How does music help define what the play is about? Who sings and why? Where should songs happen and why? So far most of the songs are about making movies. This seems good."

March 1998: Act I music workshop

David has requested that I attend rehearsals, so I'm here in New York for the last two weeks of a three-week workshop. The focus in this workshop is on integrating songs and music into Act I.

Jeanine and her music are having an incredible impact on David and Ain. David is elated with the way that Jeanine thinks and works. Ain and Jeanine have great chemistry; their wit and energy are very well matched.

The three artists have articulated a credo about how they want to work together. Each of them has an equal voice and responsibility for the creation of this project. The terms of the piece will be defined by all three of them, even though David will function as the public leader of the team.

They allow me to consult very closely with them as they create. David has described my role: "At times you are a satellite circulating around the work, but at other times we circulate around you and your perceptions of what we are attempting."

The new work is very exciting. They've found a musical vocabulary for the show—very easily, it seems. The music is rooted in the sound of piano accompaniments to silent films, but at times it is inflected with darker, more contemporary sounds. They are talking about music as "scoring," recognizing that many of the "songs" are fragmentary and that whole sections of the piece will be underscored by music.

Jeanine is able to set David and Ain's unconventional lyrics without a lot of rewriting. Anne's "rant" is set directly from the script. This song, "Seventy-Five Years Ago," is a great example of Jeanine's imagination and flexibility as a composer, matched with David and Ain's daring emotional frankness. It is an unconventional showstopper written for a ninety-nine-year-old character. As sung in the room that day by Estelle Parsons, it is both searing and hilarious.

"Seventy-Five Years Ago"

They want me to remember
Everything that happened
Seventy-five years ago.
Want me to know the reasons
For a hundred and one decisions
I made seventy-five years ago.

What it was like to move quickly, act quickly,
On the spur of a moment without fear, without blinking.
How did I feel when I didn't feel sickly?
I can't remember when I could remember what I'm thinking.

I can't remember how making choices felt.
I can't remember what my taste was.
Did I once wear clothes that fitted me?
I can't remember where my waist was.
I know I musta worn brassieres
But I haven't had one on in years
No one looks at me like I'm woman now
No one's looked at me that way in years.

I can't remember who my last lover was
I'm getting stupid!
Who can I blame?

My mouth is dry
I have no spit
The teeth ya lookin' at ain't mine.
Held in with paste
My hip's replaced
Nothing left in me is mine.
Ain't it a shame
Can ya spare a dime?
I've become some Frankenstein, wah wah wah wah, wah
Wah wah wah wah—and you want this dame
Ya lookin' at to sing you "Auld Lang Syne."
Well, thanks a lot, but I forgot the tune
To "Auld Lang"—you all want me to remember;
Why the hell should I remember?
What the hell do I get if I admit I remember?
Do I win some prize? Second prize? Booby prize?
Sorry lady—no consolation prize!
Come on everybody—sing along with Annie and remember.
Whoopee everybody—
What the hell—
Let's all remember—remember what happened!
Every goddamn thing that happened!
Seventy-five fucking years ago!

Jeanine, David and Ain produced about six songs for the show before the first workshop rehearsal. Jeanine is also composing on the fly during the day. As she listens to a scene, she'll underscore, standing with one knee on the bench at the piano. This scoring may lead to an idea for a snippet of song. Ain, David and Jeanine make up something on the spot, and an obliging actor will try it on for size. This kind of improvisational work process allows for layers and connections to be made in the motifs, characters and stories.

⋇

Between December's workshop draft and the current draft, David, Ain and Jeanine have focused a lot of energy on the development of the character of Jane. In their discussions and work the goal has been to make her a more credible and dimensional contemporary woman and to deepen her motive for wanting to make a film about her aging great-aunt. David continues to debate the need to make Jane have this "weight" in the piece, but the new work seems to be making a case for her growth.

It's clear that Jane's story reflects the experiences of Ain and Jeanine, younger contemporary artists whose careers and relationships are still taking shape. Can they make this part of the play as compelling as the story of Anne, a silent film pioneer? This is the goal they've set for themselves.

⋇

Because we've set *The First Picture Show* for next season and need to anticipate budgetary impact, we're asking Jeanine to make decisions about orchestration very early in the process of writing the show. She suggests that she will write the show for two pianos, one in tune and one out of tune.

April 1998

ACT has made an official offer to coproduce the show. Given the two theatres' schedules, this would mean that ACT would do the first production during April and May 1999 in San Francisco. We have been discussing it here in Los Angeles for a week but can't come to a conclusion. ACT is pressing us for an answer, so David and Ain are flying in to talk through the issues.

The biggest concern that Gordon and I voice is that we will lose control of the producing and technical process. It is not clear that David thinks committing to San Francisco is a good idea either. He would like to have another production, but the timing of this offer is complex. He feels enormous loyalty both to Gordon Davidson and to Carey Perloff.

We hash out all of the considerations in a two-hour conversation and finally agree that if we can keep a strong hand in the process, this arrangement may benefit both theatres in the end. Charles Dillingham, managing director at the Taper, is waiting at the door as we come out, and he calls ACT's Producing Director Jim Haire in San Francisco to give the go-ahead.

June 15–23

I'm concentrating on confirming designers for the show. David has met with about four scene designers and is most interested in Robert Brill. Jennifer Tipton will design the lighting. Carey Perloff is very enthusiastic about Judy Dolan as costume designer. Judy is currently in the Bay Area, but starts teaching at the University of California, San Diego, this fall.

Fall 1998

We've hired Jan Hartley as the visuals designer for the show. Because we expect to do much of the research for slides and film here in Los Angeles, she and I have extensive conversations about what David is hoping to achieve. David wants film to play a

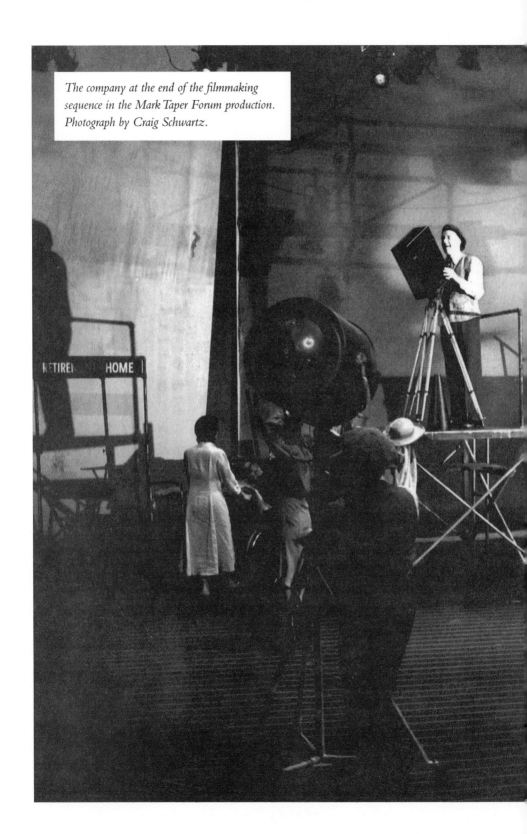

*The company at the end of the filmmaking
sequence in the Mark Taper Forum production.
Photograph by Craig Schwartz.*

substantial role in the piece. We've been warned, however, by ACT that they don't have a budget to support visuals of any complexity. Likewise, Gordon Davidson has been cautious about embracing the multimedia aspect of the show.

In Los Angeles we begin the process of finding films by early women filmmakers. We hire a researcher to track down what resources exist. After more than a week of work we identify six films that are readily available on video and were directed by women in the silent era. We also learn that it will be next to impossible to access historical films from archives. The condition of the films prohibits making copies; and, of course, almost no films by women directors have been conserved. For the moment both David and Jan agree that the existing video copies of films are the most cost-effective and efficient ones to use.

December 1998: New York Theatre Workshop music and text workshop

For the first three weeks this workshop will focus on the second-act music and on major rewriting of the script. In the last week the team will work toward rehearsing the whole piece for another sit-down read and sing-through.

It's hard to imagine that we are only three months away from a first rehearsal, because the relationship of music to the piece is still being explored. In addition to throwing conventional dramaturgy out the window, David, Ain and Jeanine have also dispatched with musical-theatre conventions. The nature of this piece has called on the collaborators to create their own unique set of rules about song form and placement. Some of the rules: No buttons or neat codas at the end of songs. Song fragments are okay. Abrupt endings are okay. No musical introductions. No final song.

December 5

David talks in rehearsal today about adapting the script for presentation as a "radio show." This will mean that the pace and clarity of the reading are very important.

Both David and Jeanine have high technical expectations, for which the actors revere them. Also, David, Ain and Jeanine are refreshingly direct and very funny.

The actors who thrive in this environment are active, not passive, in the process of shaping the material. Estelle Parsons, who has been in both of the music workshops, asks very provocative and wonderful questions of David and Jeanine. She is a terrific asset to the piece as a veteran actor who speaks out when a moment is not working. She brings out levels in the character of Anne that David and Ain find inspiring. Jeanne Sakata, who has been in every workshop of the piece, is an ideal actor for David. She enhances David's more external directions through her more internal acting process. This is also true of Ken Marks, who has been in both of the music workshops. In addition Ken's musical abilities have allowed Jeanine to create moments when he plays the piano. These actors will set the standards for the work of the company.

December 6

I wrote some notes this morning about the linked themes of independence and dependence in the piece. When I come to the afternoon rehearsal, the first thing David talks about is Anne's desire for independence.

Anne's greatest accomplishments come when she breaks free from her family and the culture's expectations for her gender, and she makes herself into a director. Anne's greatest losses come when her lack of emotional connection and her marginalization as an independent leave her vulnerable.

The overarcing theme of *The First Picture Show* is how the independent deals with becoming dependent, how an individual/artist struggles against or reconciles himself/herself to the demands of family, institutions and government.

As writers, David and Ain place value on family connections and communicate distrust for movie studios, nursing homes, organized religions and governments that try to control individuals/artists. The irony in their dramatic treatment is they create a world in which no one survives without accepting some amount of institutional support and control. Loss of independence is inevitable. The "free-for-all" ends.

Jane is the symbol of renewal. She is the younger generation, the one who acts with energy and independence to make something new and vital. Her appearance in Anne's life is both a painful reminder of Anne's lost independence and the opportunity for Anne to connect.

✹

At lunch David, Ain, Ed Fitzgerald, Karen Graham (assistant to the director) and I look at Robert Brill's first white model of the set. It is a mostly open space with a large revolving floor. There are huge loading doors at extreme upstage right and left. The stage will be occupied by a variety of rollable platforms as well as folding chairs, movable doors-in-frames and tables. Placement of the pianos on a two-foot-high revolving platform at center stage seems to be of greatest concern to the group. It seems that this will interfere with sight lines and staging, especially at the Taper, where the audience wraps around three-quarters of the stage. The discussion focuses on other versions of the revolve. It's suggested that the revolve might become a ring with a stationary center.

We have arranged a coproduction meeting with members of

ACT and Taper management and production staffs, as well as Gordon Davidson and Carey Perloff. They are in town for the workshop showing. All the designers were asked to present their designs as currently conceived. Robert Brill presents the version of the set that calls for a revolving floor. Jan Hartley hopes to have slide projectors on rolling dollies, multiple slide projectors that project from the back of the theatre, as well as video, both prerecorded and live feed from the stage. Jennifer Tipton is concerned that she receive sufficient budget for light rentals and for spotlight operators.

Unfortunately the issue of money becomes a dominant theme voiced by the technical and managerial staff present as designers talk about their plans. While on one level this kind of concern about budget is routine, this large-scale meeting is perhaps the wrong setting for it. When Robert Brill presents his set, both Gordon and Carey are dubious about the revolving ring, for aesthetic as well as budgetary reasons. What we had planned as a meeting about practical issues seems to David and Ain to turn into an ambush of the scenic ambitions of the production.

I don't think that the group is particularly aware of how uncomfortable David has become, but at one point he pulls me over to one side and asks me to terminate the meeting as soon as possible. On the surface the meeting ends well, with agreements to make revisions in the next design drafts.

At an evening meeting sans producers, the designers and creators are very anxious. There is great concern that the theatrical ambitions of the production are not going to be embraced. I leave the meeting promising to engage in a dialogue with both the ACT and Taper management to communicate better what the creators are feeling.

In a subsequent conversation Gordon Davidson strongly urges that the production remain simple. Despite scaled-back production values, the project will still cost each institution more than any other show in its season. These extraordinary costs can be attributed more to the size of the company, the expenses of a music department (personnel and score-copying costs) and the presence of many out-of-town artists requiring housing than to production values. However, since the number of cast and creative personnel cannot be pulled back, the pressure to economize falls on the designers.

I call David to talk about how he wants to proceed. David, at his most fierce, replies to me that he knows how to work with constraints. "If they want a workshop version, I'll give them a workshop version." As much as I understand the position of the institutions, I now become very concerned on David's behalf about the way these limitations might affect his ability to create.

February 3–5, 1999

David, Ain, Jeanine and I are able to schedule three days together in New York to give intense scrutiny to Jane's story and songs. The goal is to try to finish the work on Jane, giving her an arc that is more complete. We read the most recent draft of the script with eight actors and hear three new songs for Jane.

Jane as a character perplexes us all. We do not seem to have found the actress who has the wry but likable spirit that we want for her. More worrisome is the lack of resolution in the approach that David and Ain take in writing Jane. My sense is that the writing bears the mark of conflicting perspectives. In some cases the writing feels as if it's been edited down to nothing. At other times it articulates her feelings sentimentally.

From David's point of view Jane's arc is really a version of the artist's process in making a piece. An artist begins with a vague sense of what she wants to do. She sifts through a variety of ideas and makes a personal connection. She encounters obstacles and needs to incorporate them in the work. Ultimately the limitations help to give the work shape.

Some of what stops the rewriting cold is the uniqueness of David's view about how things happen. His view, that at the outset Jane is vague about her goals and isn't really passionate about making a connection to her long-lost relative, isn't dramatic, in the classic sense. On top of that it is hard to dramatize efficiently or in the quippy writing style they use throughout the play. The writing of Jane veers back and forth between being too general and too glib. We work line by line and song by song through her material without the actors, going after the moments where the writing is weak.

✷

Ellen Greene approaches me to see what I think of the idea that she might play Jane as well as Young Anne. I tell her I think that David and Ain considered this idea, but they decided it would overstate the connections between Anne and Jane. I mention her interest after rehearsal. It doesn't seem like an idea that engages them.

Despite the feeling that we are not completely out of the woods on Jane, the team still manages to have a great time working. One of the best things about the process is the group's witty and wicked self-appraisals. Lunch today was a raucous affair, with jokes flying and much laughter. Lunches and dinners serve as opportunities to debrief after meetings and work sessions. David will often say, "Now what I'm trying to understand is. . ." and open a discussion about the most difficult issue of the day. The atmosphere is lighthearted, and the good-natured challenging of assumptions can lead to breakthroughs.

March 1999

Over this month David, Ain and Jeanine finish casting the open roles, including a new actress (the fifth) to play Jane.

David and Robert Brill have come up with a set design that David can accept. The design uses the bare stage at ACT as its fundamental space. The revolve is gone, replaced by a simple black marley floor, pinstriped in white. Marley flooring is a specialty flooring surface favored by dancers because of its resiliency. The paint elevation, the detailed rendering for the backdrop, shows a huge grainy photo of a woman's face as the dominating visual image for the back wall. The loading doors are also strong points of visual interest. The walls, like the floor, are black with white pinstripes. The pianos are back to back upstage on a very simple wooden platform that revolves manually. The rest of the set consists of rolling chairs, tables, stairs and platforms. Props are limited to a few nondescript items that will represent cameras; and a large number of black sign boards and frames that will have white type.

Judy Dolan's costume work on the show is somewhat more elaborate and naturalistic, but the feeling is that this will help lift the actors off the black ground of the stage. Each actor has a basic costume with pieces. When actors move from past to present, they don simple accessories: coats, hats, aprons. Judy has convinced David and Ain, against their first impulses, to allow her to wig several of the actors, including Young Anne. The palette is mostly beige and ecru, with navy, green and gray. Anne and Young Anne are dressed in muted red tones.

March 26: Rehearsals begin in San Francisco

It's our first day of rehearsal at ACT. I drove up yesterday to be here for ten days. I brought my kids, Nick (age seven) and Ezra (age two), and my mom, who's helping me with childcare. Jeanine, here with her daughter Sienna for a good part of the rehearsal, is also balancing mothering and working. Welcome to the new millennium.

We have the "meet and greet" with Carey Perloff and Gordon

Davidson, along with Heather Kitchen, the managing director of
ACT. ACT is a great facility in a great city. We can walk back and
forth to work, up and down Geary Avenue. The rehearsal space
we're in for the first few days is small but we move into a large room
next week.

Today the company sits around a square of four conference
tables while David talks about his working methods. He first introduces Jeanine, saying, "What I do is make family. I don't use the
word collaborator lightly, so when I introduce Jeanine as a collaborator, I really mean family."

He talks about some of the research that has influenced the
piece: "To begin with, all we knew was that it would be about
silent movies and censorship. We knew that the central figure in
the piece was a very old film director living in a nursing home.
Then one day Ain was browsing the stacks and saw a slim volume
entitled *Early Women Film Directors.* His first thought was, What
early women film directors? His next thought was, This is it. It's
not a ninety-nine-year-old man. It's a woman."

David continues to talk about the connection he made
between silent-film pioneers and his own work as a choreographer
or writer or director: "In the course of inventing film, someone
thought it would last. It didn't. Those things have all disappeared.
William Weldon made five hundred films. They're all gone. And
Vivien Leigh lucked into making *Gone with the Wind* and *Streetcar,*
so she remains a star we know. Some of the biggest stars of the
moment disappeared. It's all a crap shoot."

After a break we read through the play and hear the music.

March 27

As David and the actors go through the text, David says, "I came
to the position of director rather late in life. I don't have the vocab-

Anne Gee Byrd (in wheelchair), Valda Setterfield (behind her), Evan Pappas, Dinah Lenney and Norma Fire in the ACT production. Photograph by Ken Friedman.

ulary of beats and arc and so on. I could have learned it by now, but I distrust these symbols. . . . When you want to get from one place to another place, let's just work it out from where we are."

Following up on this statement, Ken Marks asks on behalf of performers who are almost all double, triple or quadruple-cast, "If I might venture an actory question, who are we in the opening song?"

David smiles and says, "You may determine that you wish to spend the major part of this song as Billy, but I don't know . . . I'm sure you'll think of something."

David always leaves the actor with the sense that he or she is responsible for these decisions. As a director of actors David is more interested in shaping what actors bring to him than in eliciting moments from them through an elaborate coaching process. He has said that he finds the conventional directing of actors manipulative. For that reason the actor with a strong personal process does best in David's work. Ain is more likely to provide some natural-istic detail to an actor than David. At this early point in rehearsal, however, Ain is letting David establish a primary position.

March 28

I came in today with videos, including a film by Oscar Micheaux, the African-American director from whom Percy is drawn. I also found several movies produced by Carl Laemmle.

Most of the five-hour day is spent teaching songs. A decision was made last night by the trio to have Jeanine continue to teach the actors their music.

When David gets back to text work, there is a lengthy dis-cussion of the Supreme Court decision to deny motion pictures First Amendment rights in 1915. The actors are shocked and amazed to learn that this decision permitted ordinary citizens to censor and ban movies and prevent movie presenters from show-ing certain films. This control was determined at the local level, from town to town. As a result the kind of films seen varied enor-mously by region.

March 30

This is our first day in the big room. After a vocal warm-up, the company reviews the music for "Turn of the Century." David gets the company members on their feet for the first time, introducing them to the technique of shifting their physical focus and direction while they cross from one side of the room to the other. David calls this "doing things on the walk." This is an essential David Gordon technique, one that he employs to create the seamless staging that is a hallmark of all of his work.

David asks the actors not to go blank in the eyes as they do this work. "Acknowledge each other as performers. Now you see my postmodern sensibility. When you walk out into space, it is not the first time you've ever seen a human face. There's no wonder to it." Music from the opening scene is added to their improvisation, and the first glimmer of what this show will be emerges.

The rest of the day is spent staging the first card routine. The pace of the process slows considerably, but the feeling in the room is robust. As David stages, he consults constantly with Ain and also with his assistant, Karen Graham. David makes a point of telling the company that this is his usual mode and promises that he will consult with many of the people in the room. I've grown used to this process, but I suppose it is somewhat unusual for theatre work.

March 31

While staging is going on, I am using my time to look for film stills to send to Jan Hartley, our visuals designer. I found a great resource, The Cinema Shop, across the street from the apartments where we are all staying. David and Ain are very concerned that the era represented in the photos be accurate.

April 1

Rehearsals begin, as is the routine, with warm-ups. Next David does a framing exercise. The frames, cut from black foam-core boards, are about 2.5 feet square. They will have a graphic treatment that will make them look like the title cards in silent films. David and Ain plan to use frames to limit and freeze the focus onstage. In pairs the actors do little improvisations involving changing direction and practicing counterbalancing using the frames. David then stages the "Credits" section of the play based on their improvisations.

Some of the actors who are newest to the process are obviously struggling to get a handle on the style. Those with substantial musical-theatre background are most worrisome to the team. David and Ain detest the slick, commercialized style of singing associated with musicals. Likewise any perky musical behavior in the ensemble sections is squelched right away.

April 2

Stairs, doors and the five-foot platform arrive today. All of us are pleased that these items are built beautifully. The casters are incredibly smooth. David stages the very top of the show and begins to bring together Act I up to the first interview. He is using the moving staircases in the opening. After getting a sense of how the devices work, David assembles the actors on the two stairs in a composition with no apparent motive, except that Young Anne can hop off at the end of the song. The "movers," ensemble members who will activate the larger pieces throughout the performance, do a dry run with actors on board, testing their strength in relation to the object and its weight. Then David and Karen navigate the pieces to try to determine how they will store them upstage with the other objects.

I have dinner tonight with David, Ain, Jeanine and Valda at the Chinese restaurant just below our apartment house. The consensus is that we are pleased by the speed at which the work is going. Three and a half years of preparation pay off.

April 8

David is frustrated that the actors can't seem to remember their movements. After rehearsal, at the sushi bar up the street, we talk about the difference between dancers, who work physically first and then find emotionality through the physical, and actors, who often need to motivate their work in order to remember the blocking.

Karen feels the actors need some way of "marking" their movements, because the actors can't seem to act and move accurately at the same time. I suggest that perhaps they need to review without David in the room; David admits that he keeps revising the movement each time he reviews. For nondancers this can be overwhelming.

After dinner we work in the conference room, selecting stills from Jan Hartley's enormous package of research. We organize the visuals and attach titles from Anne's films to them.

April 9

Ain, David and I spend more time this morning creating a memo about the way that they would like the visuals in the montage to be treated. I spend most of the day writing a memo for Jan Hartley and the rest of the production team on David's behalf.

When I finally get back into the room, I see a run of Act I from "Mind's Eye" to the "California Quartet." There is spontaneous applause from the company. David, with a big smile on his face, says, "It must be time for a break."

April 10

As the day begins, in preparation for an afternoon run-through of Act I, David says, "You have been very generous about allowing me to spend time staging; and I know that you would like to do more in-depth scene work. We will take time to do that . . . soon." Then he proceeds to spend the morning staging "The Bribe."

Ain is feeling a little nervous about seeing the run this afternoon, hoping that he doesn't find any big problems. It's hard to evaluate where we are, because David has spent the first ten days of rehearsal staging. Acting details and the nuances of moments have not really been the focus. Next week these things will be a larger part of his concern.

April 22

I've been in Los Angeles for the last ten days. Now I'm back in San Francisco through the weekend. Yesterday there was a run of the show that generated notes they want to address today, so today I get to see a run of Act I and just a few scenes of Act II.

Act I ran one hour and twenty-six minutes, which everyone agrees is too long. The top of the show is problematic. There are at least three beginnings: "Turn of the Century"; the slide montage; and "Here I am Again."

We meet after rehearsal and then again at Jeanine's apartment to work on new versions of the beginning. We spin out three or four scenarios to streamline the top, but trying to agree on one answer at this session feels forced. We may need to sacrifice something dear.

April 23

All of us meet with Jan Hartley at 9 A.M. to see the slide montage on computer. Jan has assembled this montage from film stills and publicity shots that she and I found in a variety of libraries and film memorabilia stores. The original plan to mix these stills with segments of film was abandoned because of technical difficulties with the software she is using.

Despite this loss David is pleased. We discuss the point of view of the piece, deciding that it is preferable to feel that the images are "memory." Adding an exact chronology is less important, especially if dates tend to convey the feeling of a documentary.

Jan will do another round of work in the next few days to improve the sense of what is significant about these films for Anne. Babies, women and fathers are mentioned as parts of the visuals on which we want to linger. We talk about the rhythm of the montage and agree that the pace should slow toward the end, when we arrive at the photos of Anne herself.

We work after rehearsal to clarify the beginning of the show. David has cut and pasted the beginning. We hammer away on the moment when the trunk is opened and Jane first discovers Anne's film career. We all get bogged down trying to conceive a segue between the opening of the trunk and "Turn of the Century." Just as food arrives Jeanine says, "Well, okay, what about this?" She plays a riff and sings, "Hey Ben, I'm here at the library. . . ," a kind of talk-sung cellular phone moment. It seems just silly enough to be right. They write it over slices of pizza and salad.

April 24

We have a long morning session putting in the new beginning. It takes enormous effort, and David is a little grim about it. I can't honestly say that it is a complete solution.

My instinct is to leave it alone now, maybe wait until previews and see if it can be cut down. I worry that the montage takes too much time. Jonathan Lee, Taper production manager, has said to me that every opening montage he's ever seen in a show gets cut.

The rest of the day is spent working on the second act. David continues to refine the show physically. As time grows short, he feels pressed in every direction.

After lunch Ain gives notes to actors. A concern grows that the acting work needs priority. Time is scheduled for him to work scenes in another room. It is becoming more apparent that we have some actor issues that cannot be resolved except through intensive scene work.

April 25

Gordon and Carey come in today for a run-through. Gordon's plane is delayed, so we start late. He also has to leave soon after the run in order to make the last preview of Eric-Emmanuel Schmitt's *Enigma Variations* (directed by Daniel Roussel) at the Taper back in Los Angeles.

Evan Pappas and Ellen Greene in the ACT production. Photograph by Ken Friedman.

Fortunately he has relatively few big notes. His concerns are about acting and relationships, particularly the relation between Ben and Jane who, he still feels, don't come across as a real, connected couple. Carey's notes are also about the actors' character work. She is also worried about length.

I fly back to Los Angeles, aware that in the next week it may be hard to complete the kind of focused work that is necessary to move the performers to the next level.

April 27–April 29

The company goes into four days of what ACT calls tech/rep, where the actors are onstage in technical rehearsal for four hours a day, then back to the rehearsal hall for the rest of the day. David is not fond of this schedule, as he needs all the time he can get onstage.

The report from Ain is that the transition of the show onto the stage is easier than expected. The physical side of the show is flowing well. Having the rolling pieces throughout rehearsal has paid off. The addition of stage lighting during technical rehearsal helps define the foreground and background of stage "pictures," and this in turn is going to improve the focus and the storytelling.

On the down side the split perspective, bouncing between stage and rehearsal hall is hard on the company. No one is particularly surprised that the "acting" goes away.

May 1

I've been gone a week. I received several rewrites by fax, including a big revision that makes "Mind's Eye" a duet between Ben and Jane.

David has requested that the first two hours of today's rehearsal be dedicated to working costume pieces into the show. Although he is initially pleased with the look of the pieces, David gets quite alarmed at the sheer number of them, especially for the actress playing May. David doesn't feel that there is time in the show for elaborate changes. He also feels that the number and detail of accessories skew the evening toward naturalism and musical theatre. Judy, understandably, wants David to save judgment until he's experimented.

David and Ain confer at a break. Then they talk to Judy. Both of them say that they never intended for the costumes to have this much realistic detail. They want to cut a number of wigs, umbrellas, scarves and other items now, before the run-through. Judy relents graciously but looks worried.

At the run the company seems unfocused, in part because they are dealing with their costume pieces. In addition, moving back and forth between spaces for a week has been disorienting. The complexity and pace of the show make it vital that the actors perform the text with precision. Today they're losing important story points, and moments are muddled.

At the end of rehearsal David thanks the company for their hard work over the last week and offers an apology to Norma Fire, who plays May, for making an example of her costuming. He offers his words of encouragement about techs on Tuesday and sends everyone home.

Each of the collaborators goes his or her separate way at the end of tonight's rehearsal, preoccupied with his or her private concerns about the show.

May 2

I see the slide montage in its next edit. It's very beautiful, but David and Ain feel it doesn't convey a *personal* point of view. It still seems too much like a documentary. I don't think they'll make radical changes in it, since it's taken so much time to get it to this point.

May 3–4

All-day technical rehearsal begins. There is so much work to do in every department and, with only two full tech days to cue the show, there is truly not enough time to accomplish the task. Most affected is Jennifer Tipton, the lighting designer, who feels that she hasn't really got the time to design but must simply "cover" the show. All of her refining work will have to be done in previews.

Sound is also a major issue. Early in tech Jeanine and David realize that the actors' voices are not projecting well, especially during sections underscored with music. They decide to mike the actors throughout the show. Equalizing the wide variety of voices is a time-consuming challenge for the sound department.

As we move toward the first preview, new concerns emerge having to do with the look of the show in the Geary Theater at ACT. The intention of this design was to eliminate the formality and artifice of a set and reveal the size of the stage. The design was meant to contrast with the artifice and formality of the Geary itself. The growing impression is that the size and opulence of the house may overpower the stage picture, which is dark and rather low in profile.

David also talks with me today about the relationship between stage and audience. The rake of the orchestra seating is such that many audience members sit so that they can't see the stage floor. This is not particularly good for David's staging, since it's composed, like most dance, with wonderful floor patterns. This problem is a result of having originally and ultimately designed this piece for the Taper mainstage.

May 5

We do a run-through this afternoon in preparation for tonight's first preview. The actors focus on tuning their performances to the space. The sound and lighting designers are still struggling just to cover the show.

✹

The actors pick up enormous energy from the preview-night crowd and the pace of the show quickens considerably. The audience is very attentive and seemingly pleased but not always sure where or why they are going in a particular direction. The seamless flow of David's direction is thrilling, but I see that the audience needs punctuation, places to breathe or laugh.

The audience reaction at the end of the show is quite strong. The buzz as the crowd exits the theatre is animated. I hear people say, "I really liked it. Of course it needs to be shorter." Ain says he heard comments wondering why censorship is in the piece. The show ran one hour and twenty minutes (Act I) and one hour and nine minutes (Act II), so the length wasn't awful, but we'll need to make cuts.

May 6

We have breakfast at Han's coffee shop: five tired and disreputable-looking souls in rumpled black outfits. The yellow pads with each person's list of cuts and notes are brought out. David leads off, with a vengeance. By the time we've talked through our hit lists, we agree that the best thing to do here in the next few days is to cut sections where the show is lagging. We decide to cut one song entirely and itemize a list of cuts in numerous scenes.

We also agree that the top of the show is really problematic.

May 7

Jeanine and I sit in the sixth row and are distressed to find that the sound is not good in excellent seats. At last night's performance

I was pleased to hear an audience respond for the first time. Tonight the audience seems impassive. The play does not come across the proscenium. Some performances have also distended, thereby distorting the tone of certain sections. Technical performance notes dominate everyone's yellow pad.

Tonight, after the show and the tech meeting, Robert Brill, Jennifer Tipton, Ain, David and I go out for drinks to talk about the physical side of the show. Over the drinks we go into detail about what seems to be missing here in San Francisco. Some of it seems particular to the theatre space and perhaps also to ACT's general lighting plot, which is inadequate for our specialized needs.

More significant is the feeling that in scaling back the show for budgetary purposes, the production has now lost a certain sense of humor and showmanship. David admits that his angry reaction to the constraints may have stifled his creative impulses.

May 8

The team skipped the Saturday matinee today and sat in the outer office at ACT to work through the cuts and changes. It will be remarkable if we can get through all of them on Sunday. Those we can't finish on Sunday will be done on Tuesday (Monday is the cast's regular day off). While the team is frustrated that the short preview period doesn't really allow them to make significant changes in the show, everyone agrees that it's better to continue making small changes right up until the opening.

Ain and I organize and type up the cuts and changes during the evening performance, listening to the show on the monitor. The audience reaction tonight sounds like the strongest we've had. Reports from Carey Perloff and stage management indicate that the show is tightening and clarifying. Sound adjustments on the show seem to have helped as well.

May 9

David spends the full five-hour rehearsal putting in the cuts and restaging. David reblocks the opening using frames and signs to clarify and heighten the stylistic statement of the show. Now in the first moments of the show, as each of the main characters is introduced, he or she freezes, face framed by a two-and-a-half-foot foam-core square, in a pool of spotlight. David adds several more moments like this throughout the show.

As for the cuts, we get as far as the retirement-home segment in the first act. Even at that, it's a lot for the actors to incorporate. They are incredibly good natured about it.

We feel the beneficial impact of the day's work at tonight's performance. The first act is shorter by six minutes.

I watch the show from the balcony tonight, where one can see the stage floor and the patterns of movement much better than from the orchestra. These patterns will be more obvious to all viewers at the Taper, where the floor dominates the viewer's experience.

After five previews the company has begun to feel comfortable with the show. However, the cast really could use another week, as could the creative team, before being reviewed.

May 10

Jeanine flew back last night to New York. Tonight she won the Drama Critics Circle Award for her songs and music for Nicholas Hytner's production of *Twelfth Night*.

May 11

David works today to finish putting in the last of the cuts. There is a sense of resolution on the show today among the collaborators.

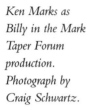

*Ken Marks as
Billy in the Mark
Taper Forum
production.
Photograph by
Craig Schwartz.*

Those in the group are very clear eyed, at times very tough on themselves, so they feel this is simply where they have to leave the production for the moment.

Jeanine and I have dinner with Judy Dolan before the show tonight. We talk a lot about how complex the shape and tone of this piece is. It has come together beautifully in some places but resists all efforts in other places.

After the show Jeanine, David and Ain go for drinks alone to have a meeting of the minds prior to reviews. Despite their anxiety, they meet to evaluate the work they've done here and to create their agenda for Los Angeles. Jeanine feels strongly that this is a very healthy way to keep command of the show as well as deal with the unpredictability of press response.

May 12

Tonight's performance is a wonderful gift from the company to the audience. It is clear from the house that the reaction is generally positive. If anything, the show seems a little at odds with the Geary, a fundamentally formal space housing a somewhat subversive and informal event.

May 13

We meet with Gordon Davidson over breakfast. Gordon is very upbeat and encouraging. This creates a good atmosphere for talking about change. The conversation ranges across all areas of the show, including text, music, design, staging and performance. Nothing in particular is decided upon, but there is good communication and a feeling of optimism about moving on.

I'm packing and leaving San Francisco this afternoon and heading back to Los Angeles and home.

May 14

It is not surprising to read a mixed set of notices, but it's unnerving to find that few of the reviewers really seem to understand the nature of this event. Most of them write from the premise that they were seeing a new musical. Few if any approach the event on the more complex terms that the artists set for them. Almost no one grapples with filmic images, with the subversive musical ideas, with nontraditional casting or with the choreographic storytelling in any substantive way. Almost all reviews focus on traditional narrative and character. Is this all that American reviewers and audiences care to have in their contemporary theatre work? On the other

hand, most reviewers are enthusiastic about the promise of the
show and about its style and humor.

May 15

I talk with David by phone. He sounds understandably subdued
and pensive. Ain is off on vacation, on the road somewhere north
of San Francisco, driving with the top down. I actually speak to
him while he is driving down Highway 1. He sounds like the wind
has blown away most of his cares. I haven't talked to Jeanine yet.
But I know she is anxious to settle back in at home with her daughter Sienna and husband Michael. Everyone, including me, needs to
take a brief break.

May 17–30

After the weekend David began to work again and has been writing ever since. I got a phone call from him about a week after the
show opened, and he talked me through a substantial rethinking of
the show. The biggest change is that he is going to eliminate the
characters of Klinkman, Howe and Slicklen, as well as much of the
censorship subplot. Later I also conferred with Ain via cellular
phone. Jeanine and David met to have their first work session on
changes in the show. I've got a lot of catching up to do at home,
at work and at Cal Arts, so I am not in daily contact.

    Just before I return to San Francisco, we have a conversation
about the cast. The revisions in the show will necessitate the recast-
ing of three roles. This is the most painful part of what is to come.
Everyone agrees to finalize the decision after seeing the show.

June 2

Back in San Francisco we meet all day in David's suite at the Hilton. With just a month to go before we start rehearsals in Los Angeles, the mood is frank and fearless. Nothing is sacred.

The rule for the meeting is that any one of the collaborators can cut anything in the current version of the show. Each has a different list, but not surprisingly, the items they all agree on are censorship, Jane and Ben, and the number and kind of musical moments in the show.

The biggest and bravest decision is that no one likes Jane's material, text or songs. They also feel they've failed to make the case that her story is as important as Anne's. The most radical suggestion, which elicits the biggest debate and the most enthusiasm, is that Jane become a direct-address character. It's decided that if she is a device, that device should be bare-faced and the style should become sassier. The character of Ben, her husband, will go.

Jeanine feels that a lot of the music is absolutely wrong for the show. She wants to remove anything that has musical-theatre tendencies, including most of Jane's songs.

Censorship takes up too much time and energy in the piece. David has already cut the citizen censors, Klinkman, Slicklen and Howe, completely. He will cut back Reverend Crafts considerably as well.

We also talk at length about production values. We agree that the look in San Francisco was gloomy and too uniform. David says he wants to restage the piece with more attention to the fun and panache of the piece.

At the end of eight hours of meeting we have our battle plan.

June 3–4

We audition ensemble members in Los Angeles. We also have a long consultation with Gordon Davidson and Stanley Soble, our casting director, about the potential casting decisions. The consensus is that in order to accommodate the enormous revisions in the show, we will have to make changes in three roles: Louis, Jane and Laemmle/ Howe.

June 7–27

Jeanine, David and Ain have returned to New York, but work continues daily between East Coast and West Coast by phone and fax. The critique from San Francisco has been integrated now into the work. The result seems to be a shift in writing and directing strategies toward the aesthetic choices of such performance works as *The Family Business* and further away from the aspects of the work that have become too naturalistic. David has said to me that he feels as if he had lost touch with his own style in San Francisco and that this time he will be in command of it. Ain calls their work "storytelling with songs" to distinguish it from traditional playwriting.

Every department is focused now on bringing the show into Los Angeles. In addition to his work on the script David is revising designs for the show. At this point it looks as if he will drop the video montage created for San Francisco. He and Robert Brill have agreed on a lighter backdrop and have decided to make the huge photo of Anne sepia-toned. Robert will detail the set pieces to make each one distinct and more distressed in appearance. Jennifer Tipton has requested equipment that will allow for much more versatility in the lighting design. Costumes are also going through a radical rethinking. David and Judy have decided to keep each actor in just one convertible costume. The changes will be simple and playful.

As we get down to the wire, David, Ain and Jeanine decide that Ellen Greene should play Jane in addition to Young Anne. Ironically, this was the suggestion made by Ellen in February.

June 29: Rehearsals begin in Los Angeles

Four years and a dozen drafts later, *The First Picture Show* is coming home. The slimmed-down version of the show is more clear and much shorter. I'm pleased and hopeful that this radical reworking will give a new energy to the work. The first act is forty-four pages. The second act is thirty-three pages.

Reverend Crafts is now the play's melodramatic villain and the sole motor of the censorship story line. Further work has been done on Louis and Anne's story line to give it more dramatic impact in the second act. Giving the roles of both Young Anne and Jane to one actress deepens the sense of family connections in the play and revives an early impulse to have every actor except Anne double-cast. Ben is now an offstage character. Jane is now a successful but dissatisfied director of commercials who rather offhandedly accepts the project of making a documentary about the silents. Jane speaks directly to the audience throughout the play. There are also a number of shifts in the casting of secondary characters, notably that the actor playing Louis also plays Henry in the nursing home, as well as Mr. LaTour.

Music has been rethought as well. The team agrees that the amount and kind of music in San Francisco skewed the show more toward a musical than any of them wanted. Jeanine did her own edit on her compositions, rejecting any music that she felt was perfunctory or clichéd.

Coming out of the production in San Francisco, she has tougher, clearer criteria for when there should be music and how it should sound. Music now has two main purposes in the piece:

to give voice to a few characters, and to recreate the world of silent movies.

Only Anne and Young Anne now have major songs. The women directors have the only song for the whole company. "California Quartet" is the only song that links all of Anne's family members. The rest of the songs are fragmentary. Jane sings in "California Quartet" in Act I and has a song in Act II that may be cut.

David, Ain and Jeanine have created a simpler version of the top of the show, eliminating "Turn of the Century" as an opening number. They have replaced it with an underscored "opening credits" dance much like the one at the St. Clements workshop.

David is committed to staging the play with more attention to it as a choreographed event. The Taper stage encourages this kind of floor work. All of us know that somewhere in the process of making this into a "playsical" some of the dance got lost.

The first day of rehearsals goes well. The company is upbeat about the cast changes. Steve Skybell, who was in the second music workshop, has rejoined the company as Louis. Ken Marks has taken on the role of Laemmle in addition to the roles he already plays. Of course Ellen Greene now plays both Young Anne and Jane. Estelle Parsons has rejoined the company in Los Angeles to play Anne. We have several new ensemble members cast in Los Angeles.

The first read/sing-through goes smoothly. Reaction from the company on the rewrite varies. One company member worries that the warmth of the show is gone. Another feels that the piece will benefit from its new form. Most are very intrigued by the way that combining Young Anne and Jane into one character strengthens the sense that this piece is about a young artist's drive and what happened to it.

David and Ain are pleased to be in Los Angeles, at the Taper, where they first conceived the show. The circular arc of the Taper stage is taped down in Rehearsal Room A, making it clear why the piece has always flowed in a circular pattern.

*Valda Setterfield as
Reverend Crafts in
the Mark Taper Forum
production. Photograph
by Craig Schwartz.*

With encouragement from Ain, Jeanine and me, David has entered this rehearsal period with a sense of the primacy of his vision for the piece. Both the rewrite and the restaging of the piece will bear David's strong stylistic stamp. This decision was reached as part of the assessment of what misfired in San Francisco. The consensus is that the script and the direction of *The First Picture Show* moved away from tenets of David's performance work in a couple of crucial ways. Primarily the feeling is that the San Francisco version of the show veered too much toward naturalistic writing and directing. This left the piece in a no-man's land between performance and more conventional dramatic and musical structure.

The rewrite reflects everyone's belief that bringing the sub-plot styles into higher relief will help the play focus on the emotional center of Anne, making it clearer that other characters function as a collage around her. A primary example of the revamped subplots is Jane: her new direct-address technique is a frank acknowledgment that she is a device. In addition, the reduction in the number of secondary story lines, and the intensified focus on selected story lines, such as the relationship between Anne and Louis, is something we have been talking about from the beginning of this process, but this is the first time the creative team has agreed on a reduction of such magnitude. This is a trade-off everyone is now willing to accept, since the efforts in the other direction have not succeeded.

At one point in San Francisco, David talked about the influence of Robert Rauschenberg's art on his work, and now it occurs to me that the piece is like a Rauschenberg assemblage, wrought from a multitude of performance styles and from the histories that David and Ain uncovered. As in those collages, there is a composed whole, but each item in the piece should have a unique truth and integrity. Perhaps it was only after the San Francisco production that David and Ain really understood how the piece could be further shaped to allow audiences to view the "chaos" without becoming lost in its many elements.

July 2

Today David works with the company on a new staging of "The Bribe." This version is faster paced and takes place on a stair unit, with the camera on the high platform above. Ken Marks goes from being Billy up on the high platform to Laemmle in the middle of the song. Company members hand Ken his hat and coat while they sing.

The challenge that the actors face is to continue to fill these moments and not simply to dance and sing. The balancing act is tough in this show.

July 4

I see a run of Act I this afternoon. I'm particularly pleased about the way that the Reverend Crafts character functions as the core of the censorship debate. It's much cleaner and more efficient.

David and Jeanine have been working at a fast, hard pace all week. The actors are very intense through the whole run. They work valiantly to execute their moves and hit their notes. This rehearsal is marked by a fiercer energy. The creators want to use their time to its greatest effect. When actors want to take excessive time to review or discuss, David can become impatient.

David creates a leave-taking sequence for Young Anne, in which she climbs up stairs that are moving, rides on a platform that spins and then exits off another set of stairs, getting off the train in Hollywood. Looks great.

July 6

I have been attending to several other projects during most of the rehearsal day, so Ain and I meet after rehearsals to talk about how things are going. Staging seems to be moving ahead, but Ain feels that the rehearsals are becoming more tense because of actor friction in the room. David is seeking some feedback about how to respond.

July 8

A problem between two actors stopped rehearsal. The company is currently at lunch. I come in to talk about how to address the issue.

David is pacing the room, worried that this is going to be an ongoing dynamic. David is not interested in having to manage the actors' behavior, but the actors feel that he is their authority in the room and must mediate when problems arise. All of us are worried that this kind of discord can derail the process.

After lunch David talks to the ensemble about his expectation of professional behavior and his desire that personal conflicts be resolved outside the room. Just airing the concerns in public seems to help alleviate tension. Work continues on the second act in the afternoon, with the room subdued and quiet.

July 20

I begin rehearsals today for a show on Sarah Siddons that I'm directing for the Getty Museum. My rehearsal day is five hours long, so most days I'll spend a couple of hours with *The First Picture Show*. David, Ain and Jeanine have all been supportive about my taking this opportunity. The schedule has been worked out so that I can be present part-time through the end of rehearsals into techs and previews.

July 21

We do a run-through this afternoon, with Gordon Davidson in attendance. This is really the first chance to look at the impact of the new work on the show. The rewrite seems to have achieved its goals and will not require major revision, only some editing of the new material. This recrafting of the piece is closer than ever to what the creators want. At least as profound a change has taken place in the staging of the play. The inventiveness and choreographic style of the piece is much stronger.

The most unexpected development is the thematic and strategic impact of having one actor play both Jane and Young Anne. For months we have been trying to develop a worthy and credible arc for Jane as an artist. Now the piece makes a direct, familial connection between what Young Anne does as an artist and what Jane is trying to do. We see more of Young Anne's work process, but we associate it with Jane's attempt to make a documentary. Of course the connection between Young Anne and Jane also strengthens both the connection and the conflict that Anne feels when she interacts with Jane. With one actor playing Jane and Young Anne, we literally *see* that Anne needs to integrate her family and memories in order to be at peace. That Jane is a less developed character seems much less of an issue.

July 25

I have been away from rehearsals most of the week, but I am here for the traditional Sunday run-through, in the fourth week of rehearsal. The only real concern at this moment is that the company continues to experience friction among various members. This has contributed to an atmosphere that is a little formal. During the run-through, however, the actors enjoy performing the work so much that the rancor between cast members seems to disappear.

The content and form of the piece feel unified at last. In giving over to this latest step in the process, by allowing David to shape the piece using his aesthetic barometer, the team has also found a nexus, a common aesthetic.

July 27–August 1: Technical rehearsal

There is general agreement that the show fits beautifully in the thrust space at the Taper. Most of the audience will view the event looking down at the floor. The relative proportions of the back wall, the rolling platforms and the actors are much better in this house.

There is both more time to meet and more dialogue among the designers in Los Angeles. Robert Brill has been here throughout tech, painting and adding hardware to all the platforms to make them look more jury-rigged and to give a less cohesive feel to the rolling units. Jennifer Tipton, David and Ain work hard to create a brighter look for the lights in this production; and they use lighting to help articulate transitions.

August 1–12: Previews and opening

With ten days of previews and daily rehearsal, there is quite a bit of refining being done on the show. Robert Egan, Taper producing director, and Gordon Davidson join the process of shaping the show through their nightly note sessions. The general wisdom is that the show still needs some cutting, work on performance and changes in the character of Jane.

Bob and Gordon's notes continue to question Jane's motives and resolution as a character. The creators have grappled with this problem for so long that new solutions seem just like old solutions. As might be expected, they are willing to do some fine-tuning on the new version of Jane, but there is a touch of futility in their voices as they discuss Gordon and Bob's various suggestions.

As previews progress, there is no question that the show is stronger than ever. The production has a point of view now that orients the viewer. The creators and the designers have a unified style for the show. The acting company is secure in its performances.

Yet as we go through previews it seems that some audiences simply don't enjoy the way the piece ranges from story to story. This rejection points to a more vexing question about the nature of this piece.

The audiences responding to the play on critic sheets are divided. There are those who seem to grasp how to view the piece through the aesthetic/philosophical lens of the indeterminate. The fact that there is no *one* reason that Anne or the women filmmakers stopped working resonates with some audience members' understanding of reality. They like the way that age and gender do *not* determine what each actor plays. They *aren't* lost when the play jumps back and forth from a linear story line to a vaudevillian romp. The audience members who "get" the play appreciate the new levels of meaning communicated through the movement of actors in space.

Then there are those who reject the event, calling the show long (it runs less than two hours) and confusing. Their lack of understanding goes to the heart of what these artists want to do with their work. David, Ain and Jeanine want to take what is familiar and get people to see it in a new way. That only a portion of the audience can do this, or is prepared to do this, seems as much of a problem as any aesthetic issue.

Critical reaction to the piece is more enthusiastic than it was in San Francisco, but few of the reviewers will really grapple with the issues the artistic team addresses. We acknowledge that there are aspects of the production not fully realized. But once again the critics insist upon approaching the show as if it were a traditional musical, and in the end they find it wanting.

Late in August, David and I meet for a drink to hash over the reaction to *The First Picture Show*. David tells me this story:

I was in the Norton Simon Museum last week looking at a particular Vuillard, and I was fascinated by the manner in which it was painted. The brush strokes suggested the texture and composition of a tapestry, a very worn tapestry. Three women crossed in front of me and began talking about what they saw, the objects in the painting, the flowers, and how they wished there were more of them. And I was kind of appalled. But I realized that I have a particular way of seeing artworks, for better or worse, that examines them as if they have their own "terms," and other people are looking for things that they recognize.

What does seem important in retrospect is how the resident theatre audiences, and especially theatre critics, do or do not come prepared to view a work that presents a new vocabulary of aesthetics. If we were showing this piece at Brooklyn Academy of Music (BAM) instead of at two major resident theatres, would the audiences have the same trouble accepting the piece? Would the programmatic profile of BAM orient the audience to see the work on its own terms? Is the "portal" of the Mark Taper Forum not accommodating, in the way that BAM is, to work that challenges aesthetic convention? How can this situation change?

Visual-arts patrons are used to a shift in their viewing perspective when they are exposed to contemporary art. They expect to engage in a dialogue with an individual artist's intentions. How can we make the resident theatre, where new work is meant to be created, as aesthetically flexible as a museum of contemporary art?

Corey Madden is the associate artistic director of the Mark Taper Forum, where she works as a producer and director. She has commissioned and developed numerous works for the stage, including recent plays by Lisa Loomer and Lilian Garrett Groag. Since 2000, she has also taken on the responsibilities of producing director for the Taper's Performing for Los Angeles Youth (P.L.A.Y.), overseeing a significant expansion of play development, production and education programs for young people ages five to twenty-one.

Ellen Greene as Anne First in the Mark Taper Forum production. Photograph by Craig Schwartz.

SELECT BIBLIOGRAPHY

Brownlow, Kevin. *Behind the Mask of Innocence.* New York: Knopf, 1990.

———. *The Parade's Gone By....* Berkeley and Los Angeles: University of California Press, 1968.

Slide, Anthony. *Early Women Directors.* South Brunswick, NJ: Barnes, 1977.

SHAKESPEARE RAPID EYE MOVEMENT

AT BAYERISCHES STAATSSCHAUSPIEL

by Lise Ann Johnson

Based on dream excerpts from *Richard III, A Midsummer Night's Dream* and *The Tempest, Shakespeare Rapid Eye Movement* premiered in the spring of 1993 at the Bayerisches Staatsschauspiel in Munich and headlined Germany's renowned Theater der Welt international theatre festival. Created by French-Canadian director Robert Lepage with the Bayerisches Staatsschauspiel resident ensemble, the piece explores the relationship between dreams and the collective unconscious. As documented by Lise Ann Johnson, the production also illuminated the special problems of working in translation and in a foreign venue with differing theatrical traditions and practices.

DIRECTOR	Robert Lepage
SET DESIGN	Robert Lepage,
	Christian Schaller
COSTUME DESIGN	Nina Reichmann
DRAMATURG	Sebastian Huber
ASSISTANT DIRECTORS	Philippe Soldevila,
	Ute Cremer
ASSISTANTS TO THE DIRECTOR	Oliver Schündler,
	Marietta Streubel

CASTS

"Adam und Eva": Excerpt from The Tempest

PROSPERO	Thomas Kylau
MIRANDA/ARIEL	Anne-Marie Bubke
FERDINAND/CALIBAN	Hans Piesbergen

Music for this excerpt by Arvo Pärt: Tabula Rasa

"Weben und werben": Excerpt from
A Midsummer Night's Dream

OBERON	Wolfgang Bauer
TITANIA	Christiane Roßbach
LYSANDER	Hans-Werner Meyer
HERMIA	Katja Amberger
DEMETRIUS	Wolfram Rupperti
HELENA	Katharina Müller-Elmau
PUCK	Guntram Brattia
ZETTEL	Michael Vogtmann
SQUENZ	Rufus Beck
FLAUT	Franz Tscherne
SCHNAUZ	Nik Neureiter
SCHLUCKER	Hans Piesbergen

Music for this excerpt by Klaus Buhlert

"Der reitende Tod": Excerpt from Richard III

RICHARD	Rufus Beck
RICHMOND	Hans Piesbergen
STANLEY	Franz Tscherne

RATCLIFF	Nik Neureiter
NORFOLK	Hans-Werner Meyer
CATESBY	Wolfram Rupperti
GEIST VON LADY ANNE	Christiane Roßbach
GEIST VON PRINZ EDWARD	Franz Tscherne
GEIST VON HENRY VI	Thomas Kylau
GEIST VON CLARENCE	Nik Neureiter
GEIST VON HASTINGS	Hans-Werner Meyer
ZWEI JUNGE PRINZEN	Katja Amberger,
	Anne-Marie Bubke
GEIST VON BUCKINGHAM	Michael Vogtmann
GEIST VON RIVERS	Wolfram Rupperti
GEIST VON GREY	Wolfgang Bauer
GEIST VON VAUGHAN	Sebastian Fischer

Music for this excerpt by Arvo Pärt: Miserere

The performance order of the Shakespeare excerpts on opening night was *Richard III*, *A Midsummer's Night's Dream* and *The Tempest*. Performances were in German, using the translations of August Wilhelm von Schlegel.

Bayerisches Staatsschauspiel program/magazine for Shakespeare
Rapid Eye Movement, *edited by Sebastian Huber.*

INTRODUCTION

Shakespeare Rapid Eye Movement (*REM*) was created by Robert Lepage in the spring of 1993 at the Bayerisches Staatsschauspiel in Munich, Germany. The piece consisted of three "dream" excerpts in German translation from Shakespeare's *Richard III*, *A Midsummer Night's Dream* and *The Tempest*. Performed by members of the Bayerisches Staatsschauspiel acting company at their mainstage facility, the Residenztheater, *REM* opened Theater der Welt, Germany's premier international theatre festival.

The roots of *Shakespeare Rapid Eye Movement* can be traced to Lepage's interest in drawing connections among geography, dreams, the collective unconscious and Shakespeare. His desire to cull dream excerpts from the Shakespeare repertoire initially developed from a two-week workshop he conducted with the Bayerisches Staatsschauspiel company at the invitation of Artistic Director Günther Beelitz in 1992. Lepage plastered mural-sized sheets of paper on the walls of the rehearsal hall and asked the actors to depict their dreams. Eventually certain geographic and architectural patterns recurred and a dream landscape began to emerge. Lepage, always intrigued by the relationship between topography and the collective unconscious, titled it a *Map of Dreams*.

Using the map as a starting point, Lepage conducted various exercises based on an improvisational structure known as the Répère Cycle. Répère is the French translation of the RSVP process developed by Anna Halprin of the San Francisco Dancer's

Workshop and brought to Quebec by Jacques Lessard. RSVP stands for Resource, Score, Value-Action and Presentation. The process aids groups in approaching collective creation in an intuitive and nongoal-oriented way. The Munich workshop did not result in performance but paved the way for a future collaboration between Lepage and the Bayerisches Staatsschauspiel.

Also in 1992, Lepage was contracted to direct *A Midsummer Night's Dream* at the National Theatre in London. Robert conducted a similar workshop with surprisingly similar results.

> I suggested that we do a workshop on the same theme and in the same way. The actors weren't aware that I had done this before. What was weird was that we ended up with exactly the same map. It had a different shape, but the elements were the same: upside-down forests, mazes, stairs. So it felt that there really is a map of dreams. As if there's a place where people go when they dream. . . . That is the unknown country that I'm curious to stage or to find. I'm interested in the people who have tried to map it out, other artists like Shakespeare or Strindberg.

For Robert the link between the geography of dreams, Shakespeare and the collective unconscious had already begun. With *Map of Dreams* as a working title, Lepage proposed the project to the Bayerisches Staatsschauspiel. The theatre enthusiastically agreed, and the production was slated for the following year.

My involvement with the project came through the suggestion of Mark Bly, creator and editor of the LMDA Production Notebooks Project. Mark had been pursuing Robert's permission to allow his rehearsal and creative process to be documented. When Robert finally gave the green light, it was for the Bayerisches Staatsschauspiel production.

Mark was aware of my work as a dramaturg and knew that I had previously observed Robert's rehearsal process as a student at the National Theatre School of Canada. The Bayerisches Staatsschauspiel already had a staff dramaturg to do research and to act as artistic liaison between the theatre and Robert, who does not normally use a dramaturg as part of his creative team. Mark suggested that I go to Germany, not as a dramaturg, but simply as an educated observer, to document this production and the creative process that brought it to life. I attended the initial design meetings in Montreal and several months later joined Robert in Munich and attended all rehearsals and subsequent costume, set, musical, dramaturgical and technical meetings.

The production itself was to be performed in German. However, to accommodate Robert's lack of fluency, the rehearsals were conducted in English without the aid of a translator. The design meetings, on the other hand, were frequently conducted in French, which is Robert's mother tongue. I also speak English and French, but no German.

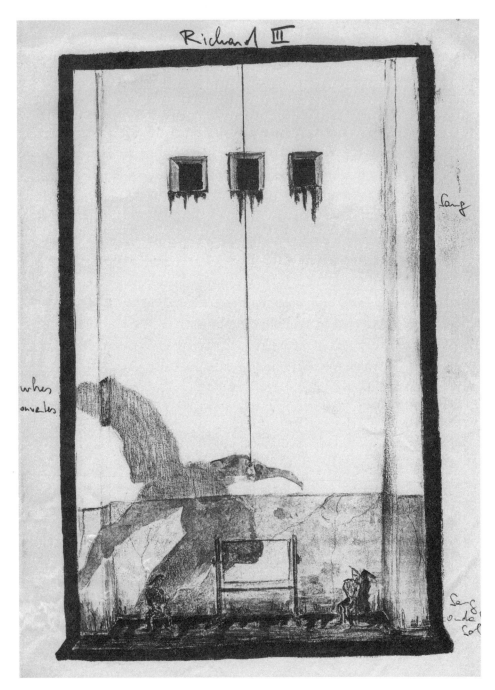

Sketch by Set Designer Christian Schaller for Richard III *excerpt.*

January 30–February 3, 1993: Set design meetings

The initial set design meetings, attended by Robert, Designer
Christian Schaller and me, take place over several days in Robert's
Montreal apartment. Christian, a young designer based in Vienna,
has been contracted specifically for this project. Although Christian has not met or worked with Robert before, the theatre feels
that his aesthetic and proficiency in French make him an ideal
choice.

We all meet for the very first time on a Saturday evening.
Robert's apartment borders the Carré St. Louis, a small urban park
near the bustling and trendy rue St. Denis. Robert arrives in a cab,
straight from a grueling performance of his one-man show, *Needles
and Opium*. He welcomes us, then rushes out to the neighborhood
depanneur for a bottle of red wine.

Robert's sparsely furnished apartment reflects some of his
interests. A twenty-foot map of time depicting man's evolution and
history lines one wall of the kitchen. Every appliance is labeled
with small white pieces of paper, identifying the object in different languages. Thus, Robert's *frigo* is also "the refrigerator" in
English and *der Kühlschrank* in German. Robert returns, the wine
is uncorked, we settle around the kitchen table and begin.

This first meeting is a guided tour through the imagination
of Robert. He shows us a book of Chinese calligraphy entitled *The
Nature of the Chinese Character* by Barbara Aria. Robert is intrigued
by Asian cultures. He loves both the aesthetic and the ritual associated with the Eastern world. We look up the word for "dream."

Robert explains how the character can be read as a picture that reveals the content of the word. In this case the word for "dream" is a depiction of a rice field seen from an aerial view. Robert is fascinated that the written symbol holds a visual meaning.

Next we look at several paintings by the Canadian artist Alex Colville. Robert is drawn toward what he calls *le vide* or "the emptiness" in Colville's aesthetic. On the surface Colville's paintings typically portray ordinary scenes from everyday life: a woman on a bicycle, a man brushing his dog, a father and son at target practice, a couple on a verandah, a woman floating on the water, a man walking in a direction opposite to that of a passing train. However, Colville's ordinary world is infused with an uneasy and surreal sense of secret danger. The human gaze is hidden or diverted, and the surrounding world adopts a menacing tone. Through the otherwise unremarkable presence of guns, machines and animals, the paintings contain a promise of violence. Robert loves the paintings. Christian finds them "banal."

Next Robert flips through a collection of drawings and designs by the filmmaker Peter Greenaway. He talks at length about the movie *Prospero's Books*. Robert admires Greenaway's notion that the entire world of *The Tempest* is conjured from the few books Prospero brought to the island.

Finally we look at Alberto Manguel's *The Dictionary of Imaginary Places*. This book offers descriptions and theoretically constructed maps of mythical locations, such as Wonderland and Atlantis. Robert points out that, like the setting for *The Tempest*, many of Manguel's imaginary places are islands. He suggests that a dream is an island where we are surrounded by the water of sleep.

For Robert an island is a place of transformation. Using *Midsummer* as an example, he describes how the forest is set apart from the world of the court. The Lovers enter the forest in order to be transformed. Their journey is a rite of passage. He emphasizes that the forest, like a dream, can be a dangerous place.

Dreams aren't clean, especially adolescent dreams. They're not hygienic. . . . The law of dreams isn't the law of society. Dreams don't play by the rules, and that's what makes them so exciting. I'd like to find that sense of logic that unravels into chaos. Dreams betray you. I'd like to explore that sense of danger that dreams present.

While another glass of wine is poured and consumed, Robert identifies certain design principles that are characteristic of his work in general. Robert wants a set that will challenge the actor. He believes a good design should conceal obstacles that unbalance the actor and render normal, everyday movement impossible. He describes moving rakes, playing areas filled with mud and slanted walls that can be ascended or descended. Clearly in Robert's mind a set is not merely a backdrop for the actor's work but is integral to that work. Robert suggests that theatrical magic lies in the ability of the performers to transform objects and space. Therefore, he wants the set to consist of only a few versatile elements that can be used in various ways.

The evening ends with a brief description of Robert's overall vision of the project. Although he has chosen three Shakespeare excerpts, he has not yet designed a structure or order for them. He wants to create a narrator figure who will act as the audience's guide through the dreamscape. He mentions Freud as a possible model for the character.

On Tuesday, Robert and Christian pin down the basics of the design. Robert wants the production to have the structure and quality of a dream. He envisions a pristine, logical world gradually transformed into bloody chaos. At the beginning the environment should appear to be an institution: a lecture hall, a school or a hospital. He explains, "It should have the look of a conference."

Robert pauses to brainstorm a list of items used in a conference setting. He hits upon a rotating blackboard, which captures his interest for two reasons: it moves and it vaguely reminds him of an island. Robert then envisions the objects into which a blackboard frame could be transformed: an empty picture frame, a mirror, a painting, a projection screen and a transparent screen for Chinese shadow puppets. He imagines changing the frame so that the blackboard could become a bed, a rotisserie, a sand box or a miniature forest. He becomes excited by the numerous possibilities, and when Christian asks about other set pieces, Robert explains that "the challenge is to do the show with only one element."

Before the end of the day Robert has placed the blackboard in front of a high wall. He states an interest in exploring the verticality of the set. For Robert a dream is a vertical experience. He briefly mentions falling dreams and refers to Bottom's Dream in *Midsummer* as a "dream which hath no bottom." He also believes that theatre, unlike film, has a vertical pull. Theatre, he explains, is

Left to right: Hans Piesbergen, Thomas Kylau and Robert Lepage work on a scene from The Tempest. *Photograph by Wilfried Hösl.*

ultimately a ritual to invoke the gods above. Film, with its rectangular screen and subtitles, is read horizontally.

At the very top of the wall, approximately forty feet off the ground, Robert sketches three small windows. Wondering how the actors might enter through the windows and descend to the playing space, he adds a lamp hung on a long cord.

Robert used a similar device in the London production of *A Midsummer Night's Dream.* Puck, performed by an acrobat-contortionist from the Cirque du Soleil, spent most of the play hanging from a lamp cord. Robert explains that he often carries over set elements and props from previous productions. He doesn't use them in exactly the same manner but enjoys seeing how they can challenge a different actor in a different setting. Several elements of this concept can be traced to other productions. For example, Robert used a rotating frame in both *Needles and Opium* and in his design for Peter Gabriel's concert tour.

We meet for the third and final session. When I arrive, Robert and Christian point out that the set has no visible entrances and exits. After enclosing the space with side walls, they neglected to add a door to the room. Robert loves the mistake. He explains that the set now acts as an island, a place shut off from the surrounding world.

The set is kept to these minimal elements: three walls, three small windows, a lamp and the rotating blackboard. The rest of the meeting is spent discussing smaller details, such as the color and texture of the walls.

Early April

Robert makes a brief trip to Munich in early April to attend a *Bauprobe.* A *Bauprobe,* which can be roughly translated as "scenery rehearsal," is often employed by the larger German theatres. The technical staff build the set design to scale in paper on the stage. The director and the designer have the opportunity to physically walk through the design and make changes to it before construction begins. To my knowledge, no changes were made to the set as a result of the *Bauprobe*.

While in Munich, Robert also cast the show with the assistance of the artistic director and met with Costume Designer Nina Reichmann. Nina had previously worked with Robert on three Shakespeare plays mounted in repertory by the Théâtre Répère in Paris.

WEEK ONE

April 22: Thursday

I arrive in Munich a few days early, bleary-eyed and in desperate need of caffeine or sleep. The city, in perfect springtime bloom, enchants me. I immerse myself in tourist culture: pickled herring and dunkles Bier in Bavarian beer halls, the hourly Glockenspiel performance in the old town square, apple pastries consumed by the swan pond of the Englischer Garten.

April 24: Saturday

I walk over to the theatre and pick up the script. The Bayerisches Staatsschauspiel is located in the heart of the Altstadt, the site of Munich's original medieval city. The state theatre is part of a large historic complex that houses not only technical facilities, administrative offices, costume shops and rehearsal halls, but also several very different performance spaces, including the mainstage Residenztheater. I am bowled over by the immense resources devoted to the arts in this country.

I discover that the script is not really a script. It consists of the Shakespeare excerpts, mostly unedited, and in rough order according to their placement in the original play. The three plays are separated and put in the following order: *The Tempest* (I-2; III-1; IV-1), *A Midsummer Night's Dream* (I-2; II-1, 2; III-1, 2; IV-1), and *Richard III* (V-3). None of Robert's writing is included. I wonder what has happened to the idea of the narrator character.

I also notice that the project has, once again, been retitled. When I was first contacted about creating a production notebook, the project was called *Map of Dreams*, an expression of Robert's original interest in the connection between geography and dreams. By the time I attended the design meetings in Montreal, the project had been renamed *We Are Such Stuff as Dreams Are Made On*, a partial quotation from *The Tempest*. Now the script bears the title *Shakespeare Rapid Eye Movement*.

April 26: Monday

The first day of rehearsal. Robert and his assistant, Philippe Solde-vila, arrive directly from the airport. They haven't even dropped their luggage off at the hotel. Despite the absence of several company members, who are in technical rehearsals for a show that opens in a few days, the room is packed. After brief reunions and introductions we all crowd around a long table and begin.

After the read-through the actors ask questions about the rehearsal process. Although thrilled to be working with Robert, they are also worried. Many are concerned that the six-week rehearsal period is too short. In Germany actors at a state theatre are accustomed to rehearsing a show in repertory over a minimum period of three months and sometimes over the course of an entire year. Others want to know about the production's physical demands.

Sketch by Set Designer Christian Schaller for The Tempest *excerpt.*

Rumor has spread that a few actors will have to enter through the tiny windows and climb down forty feet to the floor.

A longer, more heated debate about the translation ensues. The translation was chosen by the dramaturg, Sebastian Huber, in consultation with Lepage. Robert said he wanted a translation that was both faithful to the original and strange to the ear. He did not want modern versions of the plays. Huber chose nineteenth-century translations by August Wilhelm von Schlegel. Some of the actors protest the choice. They feel that the translations are too "flowery," that the translator has tried to add his own poetry to Shakespeare's images. They prefer a "more direct" modern translation. Huber argues that most modern translations oversimplify the language and don't respect the rhythm of the verse. The debate is temporarily put on hold, but Sebastian and Robert agree that the actors can propose changes to the text.

Robert spends the rest of the morning laying out his overall vision for the production, his interpretation of the three plays, and his general approach to Shakespeare. He begins by presenting the set. Few changes have been made since the initial design meetings. The rotating blackboard is joined to the wall by a small hidden platform. This device will enable actors to climb behind or on top of the frame. A ceiling now encloses the set from above. With seemingly few options for top or back light, Robert admits that the lighting design will be "a challenge."

Robert uses the project's new title, *Shakespeare Rapid Eye Movement*, to describe his desired aesthetic for the show. He wants the production to be fast, visual and full of movement. He says, "I want to give the audience the impression that everything happens in three seconds." When I ask about the change in title, my question evokes laughter around the table. Robert had not realized that the previous project title, *We Are Such Stuff as Dreams Are Made On*, in addition to being a quotation from *The Tempest*, is also the well-known title of an infamously bad romance novel in Germany.

Robert speaks briefly about his interpretation of each play. He calls *The Tempest*, one of Shakespeare's last plays, a farewell to the act of creation. He refers to it as a "Genesis story" and compares Prospero to God creating the world. He also describes Prospero as a Freud figure. Ariel and Caliban, he suggests, are the subconscious of Miranda and Ferdinand. This explains why he has double-cast these roles.

Turning to *A Midsummer Night's Dream*, Robert describes the excerpt as Bottom's Dream. He reminds us that Bottom is a weaver by profession, an image he connects to the phrase "weaving dreams."

Robert labels *Richard III* a play of opposites. He sees Richard and Richmond as mirrors of each other, one the incarnation of evil and the other the incarnation of good.

Before breaking for the day Robert encourages the actors to "be respectful of the work but not of Shakespeare." He urges them to "play, not act." Describing the monologues as jazz, he says, "Each word is an object. Play with the sound and sense of the words. Treat them like toys." Robert suggests that the words, not the actor, transport emotion to the audience. He emphasizes that "emotion is the property of the audience, not the actors." In conclusion Robert reveals that he prefers to work as a guide rather than as a director. He promises, "I will never tell an actor, 'Say it like this.'"

In the afternoon Robert meets with Nina to discuss costumes for *The Tempest* and *Richard III*. They settle on a few general principles. Prospero, as a Freud figure, will wear a white lab coat. The costumes for *Richard III* will be historically accurate. Robert requests period armor for the battle scene.

April 27: Tuesday

Robert and Nina meet to discuss the costume designs for *Midsummer*. Nina shows Robert documentary photos of Polynesian tribal cultures. She points to a photo of a half-naked man with weeds, objects and flowers woven into his hair. She suggests it as a starting point for Puck's costume. Robert is enthusiastic. He plans to build traps into the set floor and have Puck and Oberon emerge from the earth. Puck and Oberon belong to the underworld, the Lovers walk on the ground, and Titania and her Fairies inhabit the air. Robert envisions Titania as a black-widow spider. They discuss the mechanics of a cocoonlike device that would enable the actress to ascend and descend the walls of the set. Nina suggests emphasizing the sexuality of the image by asking the actress to appear bare-breasted, covered perhaps by body paint.

Next we look at Nina's proposal for the Lovers. She pulls out a photo of models draped in sheets. The sheets are tied loosely as togas. The draped sheets evoke the world of sleep and dreams, while the toga style is reminiscent of the play's ancient-world setting. Robert loves the idea, and notes the challenge it might provide the actors: "You never know when it will slip."

For the Mechanicals Nina bookmarked folkloric pictures of Greece. Robert focuses on a photo of elderly Greek men drinking ouzo in a dusty café. Suddenly something seems to click. The Lovers, he explains, are in the throes of hormone-driven adolescence. In contrast, the Mechanicals are old men, long past their sexual prime.

April 28–May 1: Wednesday–Saturday

Robert rehearses individual scenes from *Midsummer* and *The Tempest*. Although we move into a new rehearsal space on Friday, complete with a twenty-foot makeshift version of the set, all rehearsals are spent around the table.

Toward the end of the week Robert offers the actors physical images for their characters and directs the readings in musical terms. For *The Tempest* he asks Anne-Marie Bubke to use her nor-

mal voice for Miranda and a higher range for Ariel. He instructs
Hans Piesbergen to use his normal voice for Ferdinand, and a lower
range for Caliban. He suggests that "the character lives in that particular voice range." I learn that this is a typical Lepage direction.
Robert often asks the actor to find the psychology of the character in a physical image. He also often employs musical terms such
as rhythm and timbre to describe a scene. He labels the secret-
meeting scene between Miranda and Ferdinand "pianissimo" and
asks them to whisper their text. Although the actors may not
understand the content of what they are saying, the direction clues
them in to the circumstances and stakes of the scene.

WEEK TWO
May 3: Monday

Rehearsals are temporarily moved to Berlin, to accommodate the
company's invitation to perform *Romeo and Juliet*, a piece from
their repertoire, at the Theatertreffen, Berlin's annual festival of
German theatre.

On Monday we rehearse individual scenes with Hans, the
actor playing Caliban/Ferdinand. Robert arrives with a newly purchased book on Butoh dance, which depicts figures twisted into
grotesque positions. In several photos a dancer lies on his back,
reaching helplessly upward with his arms, head and legs. Robert
compares the image to "a turtle flipped on his back."

Using the photo as a starting point, Hans attempts Caliban's
monologue in the turtle position using the lower range of his
voice. He is exhausted after only a few lines. Robert urges him to
find the position that offers the greatest tension, and the actor pushes
his physical limits. It strains his abdominal muscles to maintain and
change the position and to speak in an unusually low voice all at the
same time. Soon saliva is dripping down the actor's face, and his

*Thomas Kylau (top)
and Hans Piesbergen in*
The Tempest *excerpt.
Photograph by Wilfried
Hösl.*

voice begins to tremble from the strain. Captivated, Robert suggests that "the character appears through the exhaustion."

After a break to recuperate, Robert asks the actor to find "the limits of the character." If the lowest physical point of the character is the turtle position on the floor, then the actor must also define the highest point. They return to the Butoh book and select a photo of a dancer with turned-in feet hunched over a long bamboo pole. An inferno rages in the background. Robert characterizes the image as "walking on fire."

Looking around the room, Robert grabs a long cardboard poster tube as a substitute for the bamboo pole. Hans repeats the monologue numerous times, exploring various positions within the two established limits. Robert changes the actor's physical limitations by defining the space. He places Hans on top of a small table and asks him to try the monologue again. Other times he directs the actor's use of the prop. He tells Hans, "Hold the stick like an animal might, not like a human." He offers images along the way: "Caliban is like an animal in a zoo that traces the same path over and over again in his cage." Hans tries the monologue yet again. Afterward, exhausted, Hans collapses onto his back to rest. Robert exclaims, "That's our transition into Ferdinand!"

After a brief break we look at Ferdinand's parallel monologue. Robert suggests that, unlike Caliban, Ferdinand takes pleasure in his labor and moves in a logical, precise and elegant way. In both monologues the character chops and hauls wood for fuel. Conveniently, Robert notes, the pole can represent the wood.

May 4: Tuesday

Robert is scheduled to rehearse with the Lovers from *Midsummer*. Unfortunately the rehearsal is canceled because of the illness of one of the actors. Instead Robert rehearses with Oberon and Puck. Robert describes Oberon as a hippopotamus and Puck as the bird on his back. Wolfgang Bauer, the actor playing Oberon, is a former professional soccer player with a large, imposing build. In contrast, Guntram Brattia, the actor playing Puck, is small and quick, with the flexibility of a gymnast. Using the hippo-bird image, they improvise a physical relationship without the text. Robert coaches them, urging them to slow down: "Oberon should have the rhythm and energy of a reptile. Reptiles are very still and then move suddenly, with short, quick bursts." They continue to explore, but the actors are too aware of their own movements. They seem preoccupied with what Robert labels "acrobatics." We take a quick break.

Robert shows the Butoh book to Guntram and Wolfgang. He points to a picture of a dancer reaching upward, his hands and feet twisting out awkwardly from his body. Robert says, "He looks like a tree. All of the movements in this book have human attitudes, but they are pushed to a reptilian state. Butoh takes the social human being out of the actor. Do you see how they never walk with straight feet? Their feet are always twisted in and onto the side."

Using the Butoh image, the two actors take a few stabs at the first Puck-Oberon scene. Oberon holds a half-crouched reptile position, his feet turned inward. Puck clambers onto Oberon's back. Oberon maintains his position, moving slowly and only occasionally, while Puck acts as a constantly shifting lookout. Oberon begins to use Puck as a head rest, back scratcher and confidante. Robert exclaims, "That's the relationship. Oberon is the base, and Puck is the parasite. Oberon uses Puck for his own purposes." Robert encourages them by adding and refining images. He says, "Oberon is always preoccupied. He's like Rodin's sculpture, *The Thinker.*" Later he adds, "Oberon is like a tree. He's full of knots. His legs are like roots." To Puck, he says, "Puck is like a lost bird. He needs Oberon."

The rehearsal ends. The actors are excited by what they have found in such a short time. Robert encourages them to keep exploring on their own. He says, "Keep trying it many more times. Don't set it. Remember what you like, but keep changing it and find new things."

May 6: Thursday

Following a travel day we are back in Munich, which now feels sleepy and provincial in contrast to the buzz of Berlin. The morning is consumed by a technical rehearsal designed to test Titania's descent from the window and Puck's and Oberon's use of the lamp cord to ascend the wall. Tension runs high. The technical director insists that Robert's demands are impossible and unsafe. The theatre has brought in both a mountain-climbing expert and a circus performer to lend their expertise, but the circus performer turns out to be a tightrope walker who knows little about acrobatics. Many people point out problems, but few offer solutions.

Unfortunately the solutions clash with Robert's aesthetic. The rope recommended for the lamp "wire" is very thick. Robert wants it to look like an electrical cord, not a gymnast's rope, but no one can suggest an alternative. Robert also wants Christiane Roßbach, the actress playing Titania, to emerge from a cocoon and crawl down the wall. He and Nina envision a seductive body-revealing costume. The climbing expert insists that Christiane wear mountain-climbing equipment and use two ropes for her descent. She now looks more like carry-on luggage than a black-widow spider.

In the afternoon we rehearse scenes involving Titania. In Robert's interpretation Titania is an imposing figure who initially wields power over Oberon. Looking for ways to make Titania larger than life, he places Christiane in the middle window and asks two other actresses to extend their arms out the neighboring side windows. Although the image is not quite convincing, Titania appears to have extremely long, insectlike arms.

Christiane tries her first monologue. She gives up in frustration, worried that the speech is too long and filled with antiquated references. She is concerned that the audience won't listen to her. She also admits that she feels impotent without the use of her real arms.

May 7–8: Friday and Saturday

Away from the table Robert continues to work through each excerpt on its feet. In general he searches for a physical principle on which to base the actor's work: an image, a prop, a tempo or a spatial frame. He often begins with an image that implies a style of movement for either the character or the scene. Robert suggests to Anne-Marie that "Ariel is the child in Miranda." He asks her to explore a quick, childlike voice and a light, frenetic way of walking. Anne-Marie tries the scene. She weaves in and around the stage, forcing Prospero to chase after her. Robert likes the spontaneity and danger the movement brings to the scene.

In a *Midsummer* rehearsal with the four Lovers, Robert describes their fight scene as a whirlpool: "Imagine this scene and the forest as a whirlpool. You're in the vortex of the whirlpool. The eye of the hurricane." Encouraging them to move quickly and continuously, he exclaims, "This scene should look like a Francis Bacon painting." The actors seem lost, unsure of where to go and what to do. Their frustration is compounded by their sheet-toga costumes which constantly fall off and slow them down.

Anne-Marie Bubke and Hans Piesbergen in The Tempest *excerpt. Photograph by Wilfried Hösl.*

Robert decides to limit the size of their playing space. He asks the actors to play the entire scene on the small hidden platform behind the rotating blackboard. They stand on the six-by-two-foot platform and shuffle about. Robert explains that he wants a "compression of space" as well as a "compression of time and text." When the actors complain that they have nowhere to move and that the blackboard frame cuts them off at chest height, Robert describes the scene as "a nudist Punch and Judy show," and urges them to "play in the vertical."

Robert uses a similar tactic in rehearsing the dual dream sequence with Richard and Richmond in *Richard III.* Robert asks Rufus Beck and Hans Piesbergen to explore the possibilities of movement confined to a chair. He explains, "I want to see how much space there is in that little chair. If I give you the whole room, we only see the character in the space. But if I give you only a small space, we can see the space in the character." The actors improvise with Robert as a sideline coach. He urges them to find contrasting qualities of movement. For Richmond, he asks Hans to imagine levitating. Richard, he explains to Rufus, is much heavier and darker. The actors try the scene again. This time Richard huddles in a fetal position, his body tied in a knot. Richmond looks as if he were flying. The actors move slowly but constantly, like revolving sculptures. The effect is fascinating.

Generally, once the actors have found what Robert terms "the nucleus" or "language" of the scene, he does not block or set patterns. He encourages the actors to try it over and over and to continue to change what they have found. The response to this way of working is mixed. Some actors, such as Hans, Guntram and Wolfgang, seem to thrive on Robert's use of images and physical definition. Others, such as the Lovers and the actor playing Prospero, find it frustrating not to know where and how they should move. Thomas Kylau (Prospero) finds it difficult to chase Ariel and speak to her at the same time. Although the unpredictability of the movement lends stakes and dramatic tension to the scene, he wants Robert to set out a specific pattern he can follow.

Dramaturgically the piece does not develop in terms of overall structure or shape. More actors voice their concern about the length of certain speeches or the obscure references and rare words in Shakespeare's text. Robert labels it the "too much text conspiracy." He warns about cutting too much, explaining that even if the audience doesn't recognize certain references, editing can erase the sense of mythology from the text. I am surprised by the actors' resistance to the verse. In Shakespeare so much of the content can be found in the length, rhythm and sound of the speeches. Perhaps this is entirely lost in translation.

The design process continues. Robert begins to define his use of the rotating blackboard more clearly. In *The Tempest*, which Robert envisions as the first excerpt, the frame will contain a conventional slate blackboard. In *Midsummer* the slate will be replaced with a weaver's loom, which serves as Titania's webbed bower. In *Richard III*, Lycra will be stretched over a frame to evoke the tents that house the sleeping Richard and Richmond in V–3.

WEEK THREE
May 10: Monday

Most of the day is devoted to rehearsing the *Midsummer* scenes. We begin with the first part of III-2, in which Puck reports to Oberon that Titania is enamored of an ass. Robert asks Wolfgang and Guntram to find various ways of playing the scene through the windows. The rehearsal windows are about twenty feet off the ground, and there is no safety equipment. If someone were to fall out the window, he would crash onto the metal blackboard. Oberon has vertigo, but Puck, a very agile actor, takes huge risks. He pushes his backside out of the window to imitate an ass's head.

He stands on the ledge of one window and clambers to an adjacent ledge. He hangs out of a window by one hand. Many people in the room feel uncomfortable. Some can't watch and are afraid Guntram will fall. Robert seems less concerned, confident that the actor knows his own limits.

After a break we move on to II-2, in which Puck applies flower juice to Lysander's eyes. Guntram picks up the sleeping Lovers and flings them about like marionettes. Groping their breasts and genitals, he uses them as sexual toys. The effect is comical. Robert applauds the choice, saying, "Yes, Puck treats them like pieces of flesh." Guntram has understood Robert's desire to instill danger into the forest, and he pushes it to the limit.

I attend a dramaturgy meeting with Robert and Sebastian in the afternoon. Although Sebastian has been present at most rehearsals,

Anne-Marie Bubke (left), Thomas Kylau (top) and Hans Piesbergen (on rotating frame) in The Tempest *excerpt. Photograph by Wilfried Hösl.*

dramaturgical discussions have been limited to issues of the translation and small cuts. This meeting focuses on the order of the
excerpts and the order of scenes within the excerpts. Robert wants
to restructure the *Midsummer* excerpt as Bottom's Dream. In his
interpretation the Lovers' trial of adolescent sexuality is the dream
of an old man. He suggests cutting the first Lovers' scene beginning the excerpt with a spliced Mechanicals' scene and ending with
Bottom's monologue.

Robert also changes the order of the excerpts. He wants to
begin with *The Tempest*, move on to *Richard III* and end with
Midsummer. He wants to end the show with Bottom's monologue.

May 11: Tuesday

We work through the Titania–Bottom scenes. A frame resembling
a weaver's loom has been installed in the blackboard and rotated
horizontally. These scenes will be played on the frame, as if it were
a spider's webbed bed. At the beginning of rehearsal Robert
announces a new idea: the Fairies in *Midsummer* will be portrayed
as hands that appear through the mesh. We test the idea. As Titania
and Bottom recline on the mesh, other actors push their hands up
and around them from underneath. Despite a lack of room for the
actors to maneuver, the hands add a surreal and menacing tone to
the scene.

May 12: Wednesday

We hold a technical rehearsal in the Residenztheater. Although the
rehearsal is frustrating and slow, Robert manages to find enough
mechanical solutions to try both Titania's descent from the window at the beginning of the *Midsummer* excerpt and the ascent of

Puck, Oberon and Titania up the wall and through the windows as the show's final image. The sequences are rough and fraught with technical difficulties. They are also stunning. They effectively warp the viewer's sense of perspective and dimension.

We also rehearse the Lovers' fight scene in costume. The sheets, which were meant to challenge the actor, are no longer an obstacle. The actors tie the sheets to avoid the danger of exposing bare flesh. The costumes now look more like toddler's diapers than a rumpled adolescent fantasy.

In the evening Robert works with Bottom on his final monologue. We discover the difficulties of working in translation. Robert wants to end the speech on the following line: "I will get Peter Quince to write a ballad of this dream: it shall be called 'Bottom's Dream,' because it hath no bottom." Robert suggests that the image of a bottomless dream supports the verticality of the set with its traps and high walls. However, we learn that the line is substantially different in the German translation. Bottom is known as "Zettel" in Germany. While *Zettel* is a weaving term meaning "warp," a more common meaning is "slip of paper" or "placard." Robert also discovers that Zettel is never identified as a weaver in the German translation. Robert is disappointed. He drew connections between Bottom's profession and the phrase "weaving dreams," which also does not exist in translation. This link led him to portray Titania as a spider and to design the blackboard frame as a loom.

May 13: Thursday

We work with Prospero and Miranda/Ariel on I-2 of *The Tempest*. Robert focuses on the physical characterization of Ariel. He describes her as "a spirit without a sense of direction. She takes on a body but doesn't know how to walk." Anne-Marie tries the scene but doesn't find the sense of disorientation Robert wants. He then asks her to play the scene with her eyes closed. The actress and the character become childlike. Prospero has to chase after her, both to hear what Ariel is saying and to make sure Anne-Marie doesn't fall off the stage. Their movement resembles a waltz of imprisonment, with Ariel constantly looking for freedom and Prospero desperately trying to control her. Robert is pleased but tells them, "It's still too elegant." He explains that "letting Ariel out of Miranda is like letting a bird out of its cage. Prospero goes crazy trying to catch it and put it back in its cage. It's like watching a fire in his laboratory that's gotten out of hand and is spreading." They try the scene again. Thomas isn't comfortable with improvising their pattern of movement. He worries that Anne-Marie will hurt herself. Robert encourages him, explaining that it's "moving" to watch Prospero lose control.

During a break Robert plays us the music he intends to use under the scene. He has chosen recorded music by the Estonian composer Arvo Pärt for *The Tempest* and *Richard III* but will commission an original piece for *Midsummer.* We try the scene with the music. The song gives the actors a structure. They shape the pattern and arc of their movement to corresponding changes in the tempo, rhythm and tone of the song. However, I fear the music falsely inspires and comforts the actors. It gives them the illusion that the scene is an emotionally charged and neatly packaged product. I wonder if, contrary to Robert's expressed desire, the music actually entrenches patterns and allows the actors to stop exploring.

May 14: Friday

Robert rehearses with the Mechanicals from *Midsummer.* We run through I–2. Although he had asked the actors to research the mannerisms, movement and gestures of old age, they play the scene straight. We try the scene again. Robert tries to set some comic business, but nothing seems to stick. The actors become consumed with trying to do what Robert terms "something interesting." At the end of the rehearsal two actors confess that they don't want to play their characters as old men. Robert is frustrated.

After lunch, we rehearse the final *Tempest* scene, in which Prospero offers Miranda to Ferdinand as "my gift, and thine own acquisition worthily purchased." Robert has found a way to make the blackboard resemble a large jewelry box. On one side the frame is a slate tablet. On the other the surface is mirrored. Prospero invites Ferdinand to sit with him in front of the blackboard. The frame revolves, revealing Miranda asleep on a silk cushion. The mirrored side of the frame looks like the lid of a jewelry box. Miranda looks like a precious object.

We run through the scene several times. Robert decides to alter the ending to incorporate a brief moment in Act V in which Miranda and Ferdinand play chess. Miranda accuses Ferdinand of cheating: "Sweet lord, you play me false." Ferdinand denies it: "No, my dearest love, I would not for the world." Robert suggests adding these two lines to punctuate the end of the excerpt. He instructs Prospero to seat Miranda and Ferdinand at a chessboard. We run through the scene. Robert is pleased. He describes the scene as Prospero "putting the fate of the world into the future king and queen." The addition of the two extra lines adds a question mark to the section and throws the material back out to the audience. The audience member sees not only divine creation, but also human flaw.

Robert adds music to the scene. Although the music is atmospheric, I find that it completely dictates the rhythm of the scene by imposing a slow, ethereal movement on the actors.

After rehearsal we meet with Sebastian and Christian about the poster design. Sebastian has brought in a book of collages by Max Ernst and other surrealist artists. Robert likes the idea of a collage. He suggests that it reflects the dramaturgy of the production. Christian offers to compose some sketches for the poster.

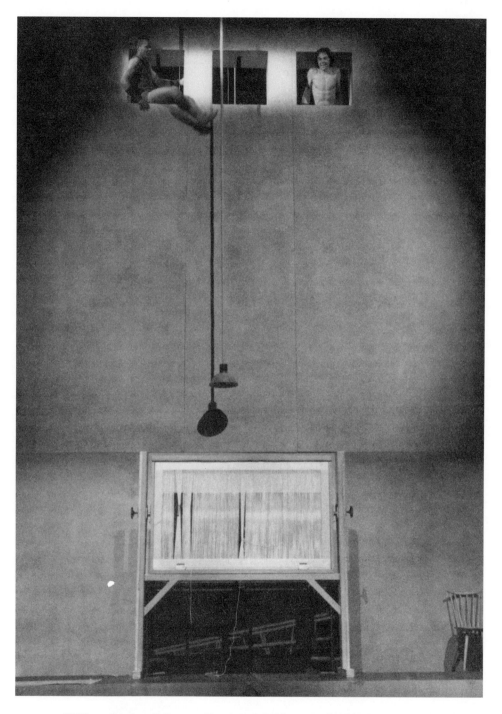

Wolfgang Bauer and Guntram Brattia in A Midsummer Night's Dream *excerpt. Photograph by Wilfried Hösl.*

May 15: Saturday

We rehearse the *Richard III* excerpt, taken from V–3. Robert has divided the excerpt into two parts: the dual dream sequence, in which Richard and Richmond are visited by the ghosts from Richard's past, and the battle at the end of the play.

For the ghost scene, set in the interiors of Richard and Richmond's tents, Lycra material has been stretched taut over the rotating frame. Robert wants the outline of the actors to emerge through the stretchy material, as if the ghosts take form in the surface of the tent. He asks the actors to stand on the small platform behind the blackboard and explore the Lycra frame. They place their face and hands in the material but don't push hard enough to create a clearly defined shape. When Robert encourages them to "come out of the edges of the frame," we discover a few technical problems: the Lycra unravels and the rehearsal frame breaks under the weight of three men. Regardless, we continue. The effect is neither clear nor striking. Occasionally, the jumble of human bodies seen through the Lycra creates the impression of floating, ethereal forms. Robert compares it to a bas-relief fresco in an Italian church.

We move on to the battle between Richard and Richmond. Robert wants to use the two chairs to represent horses. He asks the actors to improvise with the chairs in order to find a movement suggesting the gait of a horse. Complete chaos reigns at the beginning, but Robert is patient. He defines the two extremes of the rocking movement, establishes a convincing rhythm and then adds attendants, costume pieces and long swords. He sets the beginning of the scene and the moment in which Richard is killed. The rest begins to fall into place.

Watching the actors run through their work at the end of the day, I wonder if *Richard III* has best captured Robert's dream aesthetic. The piece mixes real and make-believe, authentic armor and chair horses.

WEEK FOUR
May 17: Monday

Robert rehearses with the Mechanicals. They run through their first scene. The actors have created very broad caricatures of old men. Robert tries to push their characterizations in a more subtle and realistic direction. At the same time he tries to choreograph comic business, using an ouzo bottle as a prop. When the actors incorporate their own ideas and objects into the scene, Robert stops them and explains that the blocking is too imprecise and that the bottle has lost its significance. The actors ignore Robert and argue at length in German among themselves.

May 19: Wednesday

We lose two days of rehearsal from our fourth week. The Bayerisches Staatsschauspiel's production of *Romeo and Juliet* has been invited to the Vienna Festival. Some of our actors are in that production as well. In order to salvage a day of rehearsal, we all travel to Austria. Housed in a rehearsal hall near the tantalizing Naschmarkt, one of the world's largest open-air markets, we run through *The Tempest* in the morning and rehearse scenes between Puck and Oberon in the afternoon. Puck and Oberon continue to improvise new ideas for their scene. Robert is pleased with their initiative and progress.

After rehearsal Christian presents his proposal for the poster. He has sketched a few collages, using images from the show: a horse's head in a window, a chess piece, armor, a dying bird. Robert suggests that the elements are too isolated and don't form a cohesive whole. I wonder if Robert's comments can also be applied to the show. At the moment I don't understand how the individual excerpts fit together. What is the overall structure of the piece?

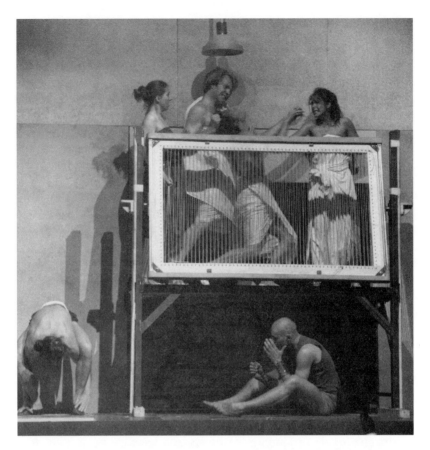

On the floor, left to right: Guntram Brattia and Wolfgang Bauer. On the rotating frame: Katja Amberger, Wolfram Rupperti, Hans-Werner Meyer and Katharina Müller-Elmau in A Midsummer Night's Dream *excerpt. Photograph by Wilfried Hösl.*

In the evening Robert, Philippe, Christian and I catch The Wooster Group at the Vienna Festival, performing the double bill of *The Emperor Jones* and *Fish Story*. We grab a bite to eat after the show. Over a delicious Italian meal and shared bottle of red wine we discuss the progress of rehearsals. Robert is discouraged by the circumstances surrounding the production. The theatre is in the midst of changing administrations and *REM* marks the company's last show as an ensemble. Some actors have had their contracts renewed, but most haven't. He fears that the changes and out-of-town rehearsals have left the company fatigued.

I suspect that everyone, including Robert, is worried about his impending week-long absence, scheduled for May 23–30. Robert travels to Montreal for the opening of his Shakespeare trilogy at the Festival of the Americas. Although his assistant, Philippe, will take over rehearsals, the actors have already begun to panic about the lack of time.

Robert also admits that he was upset by Monday's rehearsal with the Mechanicals. He fears that the actors don't trust him. Every time a blocking pattern is set, they change it and he has to start again. They are not reassured when he tells them a particular piece of business is comic. When Christian urges Robert to pull rank, he refuses, saying, "I'm a director, not a police officer." I wonder why the Mechanicals resent having precise choreography imposed on their scene. Many of the other actors, such as the Lovers, are frustrated by Robert's refusal to set their blocking.

May 21: Friday

We're back in Munich, and Robert has scheduled a rehearsal of the battle scene in *Richard III*. I walk into the rehearsal hall and note that the actors portraying Stanley, Ratcliff, Norfolk and Catesby are dressed in lab coats. Where did this idea come from? Robert had requested period armor for this scene. Someone informs me that the theatre could find only enough period armor to costume Richard and Richmond. I don't know what to make of the lab coats. In some ways it continues the clash of realities that Robert has set up in *Richard III*. The contrast of the armor and the lab coats does embody the strangeness of a dream. The lab coats also echo other psychoanalytic elements of the production, such as the institutional feel of the set. On the other hand I don't understand their significance to the text.

Robert arrives but doesn't comment on the concept of the lab coats. In fact, he gives very little direction to the attendants. He asks them to be "sterile and clinical," and not to portray the historical character. The rehearsal is very chaotic. The actors make lots of doctor jokes. Many are not taking these minor roles very seriously. They seem to see themselves as extras. Some actors don't know their lines or their cues.

One of the observers tells me that Rufus has created his own translation for Richard's speech. I follow along and compare it to both the provided translation and the original English version. The rhythm of Rufus' text bears little resemblance to the English verse. He has cut half-lines here and there. It has a very colloquial, familiar feel, which in contrast to Richmond's speech, seems out of place. No one has informed Robert of these changes.

May 22: Saturday

We rehearse Titania's long speech to Oberon in II–1. Christiane is positioned in the middle window with her giant arms extending out the adjacent windows. Wolfgang, positioned on the ground forty feet below, doesn't seem to know where or how to move. When Robert tells Wolfgang that he's trying too hard to react to the speech, the actor explains that he can't actually see Titania because of the height and angle of the window. Suddenly the problem makes sense. He is pretending that he can see her, but in fact he can't. Robert tells them to make the necessary physical adjustments. He suggests that Oberon climb onto the blackboard and Titania lean onto the ledge. The scene is much improved.

In the afternoon Robert rehearses scenes with Bottom and Titania. At this point in the excerpt Puck has fixed "an ass's nole" on Bottom's head. Michael Vogtmann, the actor playing Bottom, is impatient to know how the ass's head will be portrayed. An assistant had investigated the possibility of using a real donkey on stage but ran into too many complications. Nina, the costume designer, produces a surrealist image of a man wearing pants on his head. The pants look like ears. We try out the idea, but Michael is not enthusiastic. Robert suggests that we continue to explore other options. He feels confident that we will devise an original idea that emerges organically from Michael's interpretation of Bottom. Michael is clearly nervous. He knows that Robert is leaving for a week, and he wants the issue decided. In the end Robert suggests the solution he and his cast created in the London production of *Midsummer*. The actress playing Puck, a contortionist for the Cirque du Soleil, used her feet for Bottom's ears. Guntram loves the idea and hops onto Michael's shoulders. Although Guntram is extremely agile, he is by no means a contortionist. Robert remains unconvinced. He says, "If it's too complicated, it will never work."

During a break Robert reveals his plan to reinstate the original order of the excerpts. He wants to bookend *Midsummer*, which is the longest section of the play, with *The Tempest* and *Richard III*.

At the end of the day the cast does a run-through of *Midsummer* on the set. This is Robert's last rehearsal before he leaves for Montreal. Both he and the actors want a chance to see how things fit together. Partway through the run the technical director informs Robert that Puck's blocking in III–2 will have to change. He is concerned that Puck's window antics are unsafe. A heated exchange ensues. The run-through resumes. The cast stumbles through the excerpt without too many starts and stops, but many of the scenes are in extremely rough shape.

May 23: Sunday

I accompany Robert to the airport and use the occasion to ask him questions about the progress of the production. Robert's answers give a mid-process glimpse into his thoughts and fears about the show:

JOHNSON: How did this project start for you?

LEPAGE: I like to see how people work abroad. My interest in language has a lot to do with wanting to understand how people think. You organize your language according to how you organize your thoughts and your [beliefs]. So, I came to Germany because I don't know anything about German theatre and the repertoire and how people work here and the dramaturg system. I feel very privileged to come here and see what I can learn from it. The [1992] workshop was an opportunity to see if I wanted to do this project. . . . People were very intrigued by my approach. They liked the physical training and how I try to put actors in a certain physical state before they act. I tried to make them play much more with intuition than with psychology. Emotion isn't necessarily something that comes out of the actor but something that the actor works at.

At the same time I was fascinated by the dream quality of a lot of my work. I've never been fascinated by dreams per se. I've never really wanted to know anything about my own dreams. I've never done any therapy about my dreams. It was not a matter of wanting to know something about myself, but I am interested in how the poetry of dreams imposes itself on a lot of my work. I was curious about what it meant. Not only what it meant, but how I could use it or master it.

JOHNSON: How do dreams relate to your work?

LEPAGE: In the work that I do with actors we don't argue. We don't have intellectual arguments about anything. We don't talk about theme, we talk about poetic matter. For example, if the starting point of your work is a map, there's nothing intellectual about a map. It's the same thing with a dream. Somebody comes in one morning and says, "I had this strange dream last night." Of course everybody has their own interpretation of the dream, but whether it's a good one or

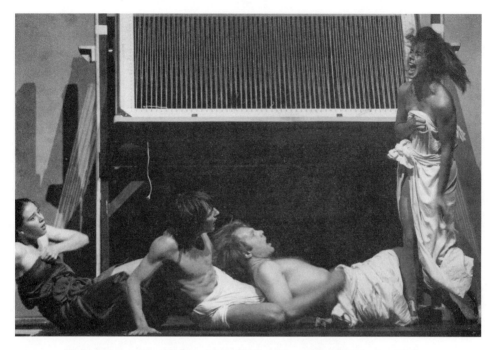

Katja Amberger, Hans-Werner Meyer, Wolfram Rupperti and Katharina Müller-Elmau, the Lovers, in A Midsummer Night's Dream *excerpt. Photograph by Wilfried Hösl.*

a bad one, or whether it's going to help this person under-stand his or her dream is not important. What's important is the collective moment where everybody has an interpreta-tion of it, and you see that there are common points. In art these common points come into play. There is such a thing as a collective unconscious. I became really interested in that because it manifested itself in a lot of my work.

So, I said, let's focus specifically on dreams in the workshop. The actors would come in every morning, and we had this huge sheet of paper pasted across the room and color felt-tips and they'd have to recount their dreams. They'd go through a process of relaxing and listening to music and closing their eyes and trying to remember their dream. If they couldn't remember their dream that morning, then they had to recount a dream that they had had at some point. We kept track of our dreams every day, and people would draw them on the piece of paper. Slowly we developed a map of dreams. It really was like a map. In a very unconscious way people drew cars all on the same highway. There was a forest and a place with lots of water and there were stairs and animals. Then we'd improvise based on the drawing. People would go away with one part of the drawing and try to figure out who the characters were and what the geography of the drawing was.

When it was over, I was asked to do *A Midsummer Night's Dream* in London. So I suggested that we do a workshop on the same theme and in the same way. The actors weren't aware that I had done this before. What was weird was that we ended up with exactly the same map. It had a different shape, but the elements were the same: upside-down forests, mazes, stairs. It felt like there really is a map of dreams, as if there's a place where people go when they dream. I've always been interested in geography, and this was another way of dealing with it.

Of course I don't feel that I've gone very far with this whole thing. I'd have to do it over and over and over until I really have something to say with it. I feel that it holds some messages about the human condition and the human soul. It's like a preview of some future work. At one point I thought that this project would be a good opportunity to develop it further, but it's become something else.

In London we didn't read the play until the last day of the workshop. When we did, everybody was flabbergasted by all the references in the text that had been in their own dreams. That's why the production was so interesting. The performers and the set designer rooted their work in what we had done in the workshop. The set designer designed his set from the map of dreams that we had done. We discovered

what the play was about through our own dreams instead of
only consulting the Arden edition or dramaturgs or Shakespeare specialists. We had a very strong subconscious and
symbolic connection to the play on a poetic level. I became
very curious about how I can find answers to the classical
repertoire in dreams. Certainly, in [each of] the three plays
that I chose, *The Tempest*, *Midsummer* and *Richard III*, the
dream plays an active part in the play.

JOHNSON: Is that how the dream–Shakespeare connection developed?

LEPAGE: Exactly. I had been working a lot on *A Midsummer Night's
Dream* in London and felt that there was a connection
between Shakespeare and dreams. So, I suggested that we use
Shakespeare plays or scenes as a structure. I thought they
could become a playground. In the beginning it was supposed to be *Map of Dreams*, and then it became *Shakespeare's
Map of Dreams* and then it was *Shakespeare, Dreams and Maps*
or something like that. It kept changing until I said, "Well,
it's not really about maps any more. The map is more of a
tool, it's not really a theme." Then it became about the state
of REM sleep, the short and rapid period when you dream.
I was trying to find a title for this collage that would inspire
everybody, and I came up with *Rapid Eye Movement*. I think
that's still present, but people are very preoccupied with very
academic things. I hope that when I come back next week,
we'll get into rapidity and visuals and movement. Those are
the three things the title suggests.

JOHNSON: The actors seem very preoccupied by the fact that they're
"doing Shakespeare."

LEPAGE: It's misleading. You start a project, and the actors ask you
what the concept is. I say, "I don't know, but I know that it's
called *Rapid Eye Movement*, so I know that I'd like it to be
rapid, I'd like it to be visual, and I'd like to have a lot of movement. And, I think that if we put all of that together, it'll have

this kind of crazy dream quality to it." We'll see. You can't give them more explanation than that.

JOHNSON: Is the process that you've used on this project different from the way you normally work?

LEPAGE: Yes, it is, in the sense that I'm trying to connect my usual way of working to text work. I think I'm achieving some things, but other drawers are more difficult to open. The Répère process that I usually use was very successful for two or three productions because I had a lot of things to say. The people I was working with at that time had a lot of things to say. It so happened that our method of working was quite new, and with the method came the successes. But that emp-

Michael Vogtmann (Bottom) with Guntram Brattia's feet forming Bottom's "donkey ears," in A Midsummer Night's Dream *excerpt. Photograph by Wilfried Hösl.*

ties itself. You've said what you had to say, and you have to wait before it comes back, and then you need to do a solo show because you have some things you want to say personally rather than collectively and so on.

People sometimes think that the method we use will lend a certain style to their work. It's not a recipe. What will come out will look like you and not like something else. That's the magical thing about it. Whenever we do workshops, people are sometimes disappointed because they want to do something that looks like "Robert Lepage." Or they think it will give them "Théâtre Répère ideas." No, it will give them *their* ideas. It will confront them with their own poetry. Some people are afraid of that. The people who aren't afraid have a lot of fun with it and discover who they are as artists. It's difficult. Because of the early successes of Théâtre Répère, it dragged us into an area of trying to understand the phenomenon. That's perfectly normal, but at one point it became the preoccupation of Théâtre Répère to try to understand why it worked.

JOHNSON: As opposed to just making it work.

LEPAGE: Exactly. I always use this quote, because I think it's a great quote. Picasso says, "An artist is somebody who finds something and then goes looking for it." He shouldn't go looking for it and then find it. It's the other way around. *Tectonic Plates* was partly about Chopin and the nineteenth-century Romantic movement. The last thing he wrote was called "The Last Thing." It was a letter he wrote to a young sculptor, and he said, "The last thing is simplicity." But you can't start there. You can't start by being simple. . . . You have to go through all of these complicated crazy things where people say, "What is this going to be about?" You don't know.

In art we have this impression that if you throw something away, it's gone forever. It's not gone forever, it's still there somehow. It's in the ground somewhere, and it will come out one day in another form or shape. It will nourish something else. We tend to see our work as plastic when really it's organic material.

JOHNSON: One thing that fascinates me about your work is that I can see ideas in one show that started somewhere else. You find new ways to use ideas. Is that conscious?

LEPAGE: Part of it is conscious. Part of it is unconscious. Sometimes I'm in the middle of a production and I'll realize, "Oh my God, I've done this before." And everyone else says, "Yeah, we knew that from the start." I think, "Why didn't you tell me?" But Woody Allen has written the same movie over and over again for the last twenty years, even though it's not the same movie.

Working with Peter Gabriel was great. He's a good friend of Martin Scorcese. Peter felt a bit depressed. He felt that he had no more music to write. Scorcese said to him, "No, no, no. You always go through that crisis. I've made fifteen films, but in fact, I've done five. If you do five things in life, you do five things. That's what you have to say. You can keep doing them in different ways." I thought that was very encouraging. In fact, my last one-man show was like my first one-man show, except it's completely different. It's matured, I've changed, I have other things to say, but it's still the same.

Also, sometimes things appear in a play that are very rich but you can only use them in a certain way. For the next play, you want to try it out and see what it contains. It's like a little jewel box that appeared, but you didn't really have the chance to explore it. They have that freedom in the visual arts, but we don't give it to ourselves in the theatre. When you make yogurt, you have to take a spoonful of it to make another batch. To me, that's an important image. Each project gives way to another project. Sometimes it gives way to a sequel.

JOHNSON: Why did you choose these three particular Shakespeare plays?

LEPAGE: I thought it was important to find three plays that are very different from each other. You want people to see how your preoccupation with dreams can manifest itself in three different plays. For example, I was very interested how in *Richard III*, although it's a very down-to-earth, bloody, fleshy, concrete work, the dream decides everything at the end.

Also, if you look at the three plays one after another, they tell a story. In the first one this God called Prospero makes Adam and Eve with both their good and bad sides. In the second part you have all of the sexuality of Adam and Eve. In the third part you have the social human being and how we deal with death. But, once again, it's very difficult for me to discuss it in an intellectual way. I feel that there's a natural organic connection, and I'm interested in how it's going to manifest itself concretely. Sometimes you realize the connections at the last minute.

JOHNSON: I'm excited to see how the show will come together when you get back. I have the sense that your dramaturgy is as visual as it is textual. A different director might decide the order of the texts and the links between the pieces before starting the show. That doesn't seem to be how you work.

LEPAGE: I'm preoccupied by text a great deal, but I'm not convinced that all the clues are in the text. Once you start to work with the text, there are human beings around it who have their own logic and their own world. Usually, when I have time to do a production and I'm working under good conditions, even the most difficult actors will find their place. In the beginning, when you suggest a certain concept, the shoe only fits a few people. But if you give it some time and you try to adapt more to the actors rather than make the actors adapt to you. . . . Unless of course you have a very precise outline of what you want to do, and you're sure that you have truth inside of you and you know everything. . . . I don't think so. It's an adventure, and we should see what the play does to us in our context, because in the end what's important is an authentic production.

JOHNSON: Otherwise it's a production you could have done anywhere and come up with the same thing?

LEPAGE: Exactly. It's difficult, because this is a world where you have a reputation as a director and you have to show where you are. I'm stuck in that process now. People don't come to see directors, they come to see a production.

JOHNSON: Germany is the country of directors reinterpreting the classics. You've been hired by this large theatre that expects certain things of you. Is that difficult?

LEPAGE: I feel like I'm in a halfway position. The commission was not a clear one. I was commissioned by a theatre to do something that would be part of their repertoire. Then it became one of the opening shows of the Theater der Welt festival. They're very different contexts. If you've been commissioned by the Theater der Welt festival, you know who the audience is going to be. Right now, the project is halfway between the two. What are the rules? I don't know what the rules are. This week I took an oath: I decided to stop trying to figure out for whom I'm doing it and just reconnect with the actors and do my show. It will have the value that it has.

JOHNSON: That's a good approach.

LEPAGE: Yeah, but it's difficult to stick to that, because you bump into all the budget people and all the administrators and then the artistic director of the Theater der Welt. The difficult thing about this project is that one day I sat down with Renate Klett. She's the artistic director of the festival and used to be the most important theatre writer in the country. She got interested in my work a long time ago. She's the one

*Wolfgang Bauer
(Oberon) with
Guntram Brattia
(Puck) on his back in
A Midsummer
Night's Dream
excerpt. Photograph
by Wilfried Hösl.*

who brought *The Dragon's Trilogy* to Germany the first time.
She's very important to me. I owe her a lot. She's the one
who wanted me to open the festival.

So, one morning when I was here for the *Bauprobe*,
I did this interview with her because she needed to write
something about the show for the festival program. She wanted
me to describe what the show was going to be about, where
the idea came from, what I wanted to do with the three
Shakespeare excerpts. I explained the whole concept to her:
Ariel being in Miranda, and Caliban in Ferdinand, and what
I'd based it on, and all of that. She was completely flabber-
gasted. She said, "Why hasn't anyone ever thought of that?"
She was completely enthusiastic to the point where I thought,

Well, I don't need to do the show anymore. Now I have to do the demonstration of it. I might not be able to do the demonstration of it in as clear a way as I could explain it.

Do you see what I mean? People here need theatre for reasons that are not the same as the audience's. People want theatre to change their way of seeing things. They want theatre so that they can theorize, so that they can confirm their theories. I'm not sure that's what I want to do.

The other evening I was talking to Peter Gabriel, and he said, "How are you?" and I said, "Oh, well, the work is kind of difficult here in Munich." He said, "Why?" and I tried to explain the concept to him and the conditions and all of that. He said, "You know what? Shakespeare's dead." I said, "No, he's not dead," and tried to have this point of view that Shakespeare's still alive. And he said, "No, he's dead. Why don't you write your own stuff?" I replied, "I do, but there's only a certain amount you can say, and there are so many interesting projects around." That's the Canadian colonized attitude: to think that life's for learning. You keep going to school until you're sixty. That's why you say yes to all these projects, because you're going to learn about that, you're going to get to work with this person, you're going to travel. In fact, maybe you should be doing your own thing.

JOHNSON: At an earlier point you were planning to write a character for the show. What happened to that?

LEPAGE: That was going to be Prospero. He was going to give more info about the whole show. That was more a part of *A Map of Dreams*. It doesn't really fit anymore. I'm trying to see how I could bring it back in, but . . . I was struck by this man who wrote about the geography of dreams in your house and how one-third of the rooms in a house are for dreaming. Even one-third of your wardrobe is for sleeping. A home is organized for sleep and for dreams. It's in our geography.

JOHNSON: How did it change from maps to *Rapid Eye Movement*? It was still in the realm of *A Map of Dreams* at the design meeting. Was it the focus on Shakespeare or the time or the context?

LEPAGE: I think maybe it's something that we solved in the design too early: the verticality. A dream is a vertical thing. When you dream, there's a vertical pole that goes through you, and I wanted to explore that territory. Also, theatre is a vertical thing. I don't know. I guess at the time we wanted to create something that was blank so that we could fill it in afterward. But it's difficult. I've never encountered so many technical problems: lifting people up, having them go from one window to another. I feel that we're so safe, this whole geography is not being used yet. Of course, once the lighting comes into play it will be used much more. I intend to use shadows and light on the walls. That should work, but physically, we're still stuck in a bottom-and-top relationship. When the verticality does happen, people are so panicked and scared. They complain. Maybe it's a good thing that the complaining happened so early. Hopefully this week they'll work at it and see that it's not that complicated.

WEEK FIVE

May 24–30: In rehearsals without Robert

Robert requests that a voice coach be hired to work with the actors during his absence. The theatre hires Ute Cremer. Ute focuses on the text while Philippe takes over blocking rehearsals. It's a frustrating week for all concerned. With Robert gone, the actors show their panic and frustration. Few of the scenes grow in any substantial way. The rehearsals are often confusing. The actors don't always know who is directing: they themselves? Philippe? Ute?

Ute also works individually with most of the actors during the week. She focuses on developing realistic characterization and finding objectives to attach to Robert's staging. Although she respects Robert's direction, it turns out that she is not a voice coach but rather an acting coach with Strasberg training. I wonder if her Method approach clashes with Robert's philosophy of acting. On the other hand, a few of the actors manage to develop their characters in greater detail. In particular, Michael creates a touching portrayal of Bottom as an eccentric old man.

Technically a few old problems are solved and a few new problems arise. The good news is that Philippe finds a simple way for Puck to reinstate his window blocking with minimal but secure safety equipment. The bad news is that the construction of the set is completed and we discover that the size of the windows and the platform behind the blackboard is slightly smaller than the rehearsal versions. The change in size makes the staging more difficult for the actors.

We end the week with a mostly disastrous run-through. Many of the actors don't know their cues or the running order of the scenes.

WEEK SIX
June 1: Tuesday

Robert returns from Montreal. Tension is high. We have a week and a half left before the opening.

The Mechanicals rebel. Hans and Rufus tell Robert that the scene is not working. "It's not funny," they say. They resent the slow rhythm imposed by playing old men: "The rhythm is like chewing gum." They feel disconnected from the other *Midsummer* scenes, which run at a frenetic and sexually charged pace.

Robert likes the contrast. "The two rhythms must be differ-ent. In most productions the Mechanicals are fast and the Lovers are slow and whiney. I'm offering the opposite. It's much more interesting and more of a surprise. "The actors disagree. Robert discusses the issue of trust. If they don't trust him or the idea, then nothing will work.

Oberon wants an extra rope to hold onto during the final ascent up the wall. He has been losing sleep from recurring dreams of falling.

During the dinner break Robert meets with Klaus Buhlert, who has composed different "themes" for each group of charac-ters in *Midsummer*: the Mechanicals, the Fairy Kingdom and the Lovers. Rather than mixing the tape according to a series of set cues, Robert asks if the tracks can be mixed live. The spontaneity and danger of live sound appeals to him. He wants music that is "anarchic and occasionally discordant." Robert asks when the music will be ready to use. He wants "to feed the actors music . . . to help them understand the overall tone of the piece."

Michael Vogtmann (Bottom) and Christiane Roßbach (Titania) in A Midsummer Night's Dream *excerpt. Photograph by Wilfried Hösl.*

June 4: Friday

Robert sets lighting cues in the morning. The lighting problems that Robert initially described as "a challenge" seem more like a headache. Given the enclosed set, it's very difficult to create any kind of intimacy, isolation or depth. There is no top light and no back light. Robert's solutions, to use footlights for *Richard III* and spotlights for *Midsummer*, solve some but not all the problems.

Robert has added two new visual elements to the *Midsummer* excerpt: a projection of a forest and a film of a spider spinning a web. Both are projected in large scale on the back wall. The effect of the film is breathtaking. The gigantic spider dislocates your sense of proportion. The windows, with their blue cyclorama background, look as if they were floating. I can imagine Titania crawling down the wall.

In the afternoon Robert announces his plan to restage the fight scene with the four Lovers. He had hoped that something "interesting" would develop from confining their playing space to the small platform behind the blackboard but, he notes, "It's not helping you at all." The Lovers are relieved.

Robert restages the scene almost entirely on the ground, using the traps in the floor as the defining focus. To date the traps have been used only as entrances and exits for Wolfgang and Guntram. Now the Lovers will throw and push each other into the holes, only to be rudely bounced out again by Puck and Oberon. The rehearsal proceeds quite smoothly. The actors are thrilled to have more room to play the scene. The effect is comic, and the logic of the action is clearer. The movements support the text, and the text makes more sense. The traps also pull Puck and Oberon into the scene as participants. In the old blocking they used to perch on top of the blackboard as observers. Now they appear in the middle of the scene, watching, participating and fighting with each other. Their heads pop up and down out of the traps, an echo of Robert's original Punch and Judy image.

Over dinner we look at the finalized poster design. In the end Sebastian found a Man Ray photocollage that captured the notion of rapid eye movement perfectly: a metronome with an eye attached to its pendulum. A graphic designer took the image and placed it against a background of a stormy sky. It looks great. Robert applauds the poster.

June 5: Saturday

We run through *Midsummer* on stage. Many technical and design elements are added for the first time: full costume, music, film, projection and lighting. The run-through, although technically smoother, maintains a very constant rhythm. The music seems to flatten out the pace. When Robert describes the style and rhythm of the production, he uses such words as anarchic, frenetic, sexual, crazy, wild, spontaneous, dangerous. The production, however, feels very measured. There are many factors that contribute to the slow pace. The less secure the actors feel, the more conservative they become. The technical problems and their solutions hinder the action. Perhaps it's also the structure. We have yet to find a throughline.

Robert, Sebastian and I meet over dinner to discuss titles for each of the three excerpts. Robert would like to project the titles onto the back wall at the start of each segment. He reels off his suggestions. For *The Tempest*: "The Chess Game," "Black and White," "Good and Evil," "Adam and Eve." For *Midsummer*: "Bottom's Dream." For *Richard III*: "The Tent." Sebastian likes the more enigmatic ones, such as "The Chess Game." He worries that "Adam and Eve" attempts to explain a concept to the audience. On the other hand I like the chronology suggested by "Adam and Eve." It helps me understand why *The Tempest* begins the play. I suggest that the arc of the play is from Adam and Eve toward the apocalypse of

Guntram Brattia (Puck) in A Midsummer Night's Dream *excerpt. Photograph by Wilfried Hösl.*

Richard III. Midsummer, which deals with adolescence and old age, falls in the middle.

We brainstorm apocalypse-related titles for *Richard III*, and eventually remember the horse imagery attached to the riders of the apocalypse. The title we hit upon is "Death Riding a Horse," translated into German as "Der reitende Tod." Finding a title for the *Midsummer* excerpt proves more difficult. "Bottom's Dream" is ruled out. The German equivalent would have to use Bottom's translated name, which would impart a different meaning to the title. Robert asks for a phrase that incorporates spider imagery. Sebastian suggests "Weben und werben," which translates as "To Weave and to Woo." Robert agrees.

After dinner Robert meets with the Mechanicals. He makes a large cut in their section, reorders the material and then reworks the scene. They concentrate on comic timing rather than on establishing the slow rhythm of older men. The actors are happy with the changes. The cuts and order shuffle help the pace of the Mechanicals' section, but effectively jettison Robert's vision of *Midsummer* as Bottom's Dream. Week number six has turned into a week of compromises.

June 7: Monday

We enter the final week of rehearsals and the first week of performance. Opening night is only four days away. Robert devotes mornings and afternoons to run-throughs on the stage.

On Monday evening we look at selected *Midsummer* scenes in order to perfect the conventions of the Fairy "hands" and Bottom's donkey "ears." In particular we try to figure out how Bottom can climb up onto the blackboard without Puck having to disengage himself from Michael's shoulders. Whenever this happens, the illusion of Bottom's "ears" is broken. Robert asks if they can move onto the frame as a unit. He works with Michael and Guntram for about half an hour, trying out both his own suggestions and those of the actors and onlookers. Finally Philippe suggests that the pair approach the blackboard while walking backward, keeping their faces to the audience. Guntram hooks himself onto the blackboard first, and the frame begins a single revolution. With Puck now at the top of the frame, Michael hooks himself on to the bottom as it continues to move. The movement lifts them off the ground and Bottom looks as if he is flying. Robert loves the image. He makes only minor adjustments: "Turn your feet that way. . . . See if it's easier to hold the board this way."

After rehearsal Philippe suggests that tonight was more typical of Robert's way of working: collaborating with actors and observers on a sequence of movements based around a prop, object or set piece resulting in the construction of a visual story.

June 8: Tuesday

We run through the play. Watching from the house, I try to pin-point the production's major dilemmas. I emerge with two cul-prits: the dramaturgy and the set. In my opinion, the production lacks a framework. How do the pieces fit together? What is our journey through the evening? Where should the spectator start, and where does he end? Robert's initial idea of creating a Freud figure to guide us through this murky dreamscape could have offered the production a cohesive arc. He also evoked the idea of "collage" but didn't apply it to his selection of text. At the moment, *REM* is not a collage, but simply a collection of three edited Shakespeare excerpts that follow each other in a linear fashion.

In the end the set creates problems rather than challenges. The verticality, the predominant element of the set, presents very difficult technical challenges that aren't met by either the designer or the theatre. Both the problems and their technical solutions are unwieldy. The traps are treacherous, the exits out the side walls break the illusion of a cloistered space, the heads and hands of tech-nicians can be seen helping actors in and out of the windows, the light fixture bashes awkwardly against the wall, the light cord looks like a gym rope and the raising of the light up and down so that Titania can enter down the wall is both jerky in movement and completely unconnected to any action in the play. Aside from the safety issues and technical problems, the set also lacks depth of play-ing space, which makes it difficult to play the vertical line effec-tively. To boot the set is in very bad shape. You can see the con-struction seams, the wall is stained from footprints and certain sections are looking rather battered.

June 9: Wednesday

Following an afternoon run, a debate ensues between Artistic Director Günther Beelitz and Lepage. Beelitz suggests switching the order of the excerpts and/or the placement of the intermission. At the moment the running order is *The Tempest, Midsummer,* intermission and *Richard III.* Beelitz feels that the overall rhythm is sluggish and that the intermission comes far too late in the evening. He suggests either placing the intermission after *The Tempest* or moving the longest section, *Midsummer,* to the end of the show so that the intermission falls at the midpoint of the evening. Lepage disagrees. He doesn't want to end with *Midsummer,* which he sees as the heart of the show. He feels that culminating with the happy, almost cute, tone of the *Midsummer* excerpt would "let the audience off the hook" with a typical "I woke up and it was all a dream" ending. He also points out that it would be unfair and technically difficult to ask Hans to perform *The Tempest* and *Richard III* back to back.

Beelitz and Sebastian then propose swapping *Richard III* and *The Tempest.* Prospero's monologue, they argue, is the perfect ending to the evening. Initially Lepage disagrees. He sees *The Tempest* as a prologue and *Richard III* as an epilogue. We break for dinner. When we reconvene, Robert has changed his mind. He wonders if *Richard III's* faster pace and strange juxtapositions might engage the audience off the top of the show. He agrees to switch the order for this evening's run.

I don't like the new order. Wrapping up with Prospero's famous "Our revels now are ended" monologue seems appropriate, but other elements are lost in the switch. For example, the set loses its logic. *The Tempest* is the one excerpt that firmly establishes the setting of an institution. The blackboard is a blackboard, the light fixture is a light, and there is no apparent way to enter or exit the room. In Robert's initial conception of the production, this pristine reality should unravel into chaos. Without *The Tempest* to establish the conventions, our movement through the dream world of the play seems random.

The order change also doesn't take into account Robert's chronological vision of the structure. *The Tempest* excerpt, now entitled "Adam and Eve," was conceptualized as a creation story. Robert imagined Prospero as God and Ferdinand and Miranda as the first man and woman. In contrast, *Richard III*, now entitled "Death Riding a Horse," has apocalyptic overtones.

Regardless, Robert decides to maintain the new order. He finds the rhythm and pace of the evening vastly improved and points out that the placement of Prospero's monologue at the end is "more moving."

In a discussion following the run Beelitz questions the fight scene with the four Lovers. He suggests that it's not "erotic enough." Lepage agrees and explains, "It's because I staged it." He adds, "I've imprisoned us in this set. Because these actors like security, I had to stage it. I know it doesn't work. It's too safe." Robert had hoped the costumes would add a sense of sexual danger to the scene, but the sheets are now tied so tightly and neatly that they can't possibly slip during the entire show.

June 10: Thursday

A performance of another show is canceled and *REM* is unexpectedly scheduled as a replacement. The response after the intermission is favorable. Robert had asked the four Lovers to use their staging as only a guideline, to loosen their costumes, and to embrace the chaos of the scene. The note, combined with preview-night nerves, makes the scene more engaging, more comic, and communicates their humiliation more strongly. The moves are less predictable, and at certain points the togas even slip, revealing flashes of nudity. This seems to heighten the stakes of the scene.

Hans Piesbergen, Franz Tscherne and Katja Amberger in Richard III *excerpt. Photograph by Wilfried Hösl.*

The Mechanicals scene, although carelessly executed, gets a round of applause.

We return to our seats for the final section. *The Tempest* feels extremely slow. At the end of the show the audience response is muted. Perhaps this is partly due to the ragged, unstaged curtain call. The actors return unenthusiastically to the stage, as if they are mourners in a funeral procession.

June 11: Friday

The show premieres as part of the theatre's season. The performance is warmly received.

June 12: Saturday

Today is the premiere for the Theater der Welt festival. Although no rehearsals are scheduled during the day, the show continues to grow between Friday and Saturday nights. *Midsummer* is by far the strongest section. The rhythm is tighter and the actors are looser. They are beginning to play.

June 13: Sunday

I browse through the entries in my production journal. Robert's original vision of the project first emerged in the design meetings held in Montreal. Looking back over the past four months, I am struck by which of those ideas were realized, which ones were completely lost, and which ones simply didn't work.

Robert began with the image of an island. He suggested that a dream, like an island, is an isolated and dangerous place of transformation. In his view the journey of a dream begins in a safe, logical and clean environment and is gradually transformed by surreal chaos. He hoped that we would witness this transformation through gradual changes in the use of the set. In reality this journey is lost, or perhaps even reversed, with the order change of the excerpts. Also, the illusion of the set as an island, as a self-contained space without visible entrances and exits onto the outside world, is never maintained. The attendants in *Richard III* enter through hidden doors in the side walls within the first two minutes of the production.

Robert also emphasized the need to use only a few elements in many different ways. This goal was achieved. The only scenic elements added during the rehearsal period were two wooden chairs. Otherwise the entire production is played using the traps, the blackboard and the three windows. The blackboard remains the central focus and is used to suggest a blackboard, a jewelry box, a weaver's loom, a tent and more.

Robert had hoped that these few elements could challenge the actors. He wanted all props, blocking and costumes to provide obstacles for the actor to overcome. In certain cases, such as the chairs in *Richard III*, this theory works well. In other cases, such as the Lovers' toga costumes, the actors are more frustrated than challenged. In general, Robert's methods of working appealed to actors who enjoyed improvisation and could mine emotional depth from a physical image. Actors who wanted to repeat a pattern of blocking or who needed to work with text-based intentions were lost in Robert's physical approach. The perceived lack of rehearsal time may have aggravated actors' insecurities.

Robert's final stated goal was to create an aesthetic that could be described as rapid eye movement. Robert wanted the production to be "rapid, visual and full of movement." Curiously, the most powerful theatrical moments are not rapid but slowed down and imbued with stillness. These moments more closely resemble the Alex Colville paintings presented at the design meeting than they do the title of the show. Puck, Oberon and Titania's lengthy exit up the wall and through the windows at the end of the *Midsummer* excerpt is mesmerizing. Similarly, the disturbing silence at the end of Richmond's monologue in *Richard III* unsettles the audience. Even the violent and quick movements effected by Anne-Marie, first as Miranda and then as Ariel, are underscored by music that adds an oddly drawn-out quality to the scene. The power of these scenes lies not in their rapidity of movement but rather in their ability to unfold the transformation of one thing into another. Ariel is released from Miranda through her recounting of the storm. Caliban collapses into Ferdinand. Puck, Oberon and Titania disappear along with Bottom's Dream. Richmond becomes the world's next tyrant. Ultimately it is in these moments of slow transformation that I grasp why the poetry of dreams imposes itself on much of Robert's work.

June 14: Monday

The reviews have appeared. Although the audience response seemed positive, the show has garnered criticism from the press.

Predictably, reviewers attack the production for lack of substance. Many commend the striking imagery but suggest that Lepage had little to say about either dreams or their connection to Shakespeare.

The criticism, while accurate, is also somewhat misleading. Although known as an auteur-director, Lepage self-admittedly functions best as a guide who draws surprising connections among disparate elements. His strength is not necessarily in intellectual concept but rather in recognizing "the collective moment." During the interview I conducted with Robert, he stated:

> What's important is the collective moment where everybody has an interpretation of it, and you see that there are common points. In art these common points come into play. There is such a thing as a collective unconscious. I became really interested in that because it manifested itself in a lot of my work.

Without multiple interpretations that lead to common points, the "unknown territory" of the collective unconscious proved elusive.

Robert may have fared better with a collective base of actors willing to work in an intuitive, nonintellectual way. Unfortunately the Bayerisches Staatsschauspiel was not the best playground for Robert's experiment. Although the theatre possessed impressive technical facilities to more or less execute Robert's large-scale images, the basic working conditions did not match the true intent of the project. The Bayerisches Staatsschauspiel's resident company was accustomed to working together, but as an ensemble, not as a collective. Few actors were versed in a collaborative approach that favored physical work over psychological work. The added pressures of time and the high profile of headlining the Theater der Welt festival ensured that most actors were understandably far more concerned with product than process.

It is also possible that the subject of dreams proved too slip-

Rufus Beck as Richard in Richard III *excerpt. Photograph by Wilfried Hösl.*

pery for collective interpretation. Or perhaps difficulties and differences in the Shakespeare translation ultimately left Robert's understanding of the text disconnected from the German version. In any case, I must conclude that Robert's search for the collective unconscious would have been better served in a familiar collaborative environment and not within the traditionally hierarchical structure of a large German institution.

Lise Ann Johnson is a Canadian freelance director and dramaturg. She has worked for The Great Canadian Theatre Company, Alberta Theatre Projects, Playwrights' Workshop Montreal, the Centre des auteurs dramatiques, Ships' Company Theatre, Theatre Lac Brome, The Shaw Festival, The Canadian Stage Company and CBC Radio. She is currently the Artistic Associate responsible for new play development at the National Arts Centre in Ottawa. Lise Ann also teaches in the Playwriting Section at the National Theatre School of Canada.

BIBLIOGRAPHY

Aria, Barbara. *The Nature of the Chinese Character.* New York: Simon and
 Schuster, 1991.
Manguel, Alberto. *The Dictionary of Imaginary Places.* New York:
 Macmillan, 1980.

In The Blood

AT THE JOSEPH PAPP PUBLIC THEATER/

NEW YORK SHAKESPEARE FESTIVAL

by John Dias

For their third production of Suzan-Lori Parks's work in six years, The Joseph Papp Public Theater/New York Shakespeare Festival in New York City chose her new play, *In the Blood*. Inspired by Nathaniel Hawthorne's famous heroine, Hester Prynne, Parks created the portrait of Hester, La Negrita, a contemporary homeless single mother of five. Known for her boldly nontraditional and highly theatrical storytelling, Parks participated in rehearsals, actively shaping her text as needed. This production opened in November 1999, directed by David Esbjornson. John Dias, then the Public's literary director, now an associate producer, served as production dramaturg and created this notebook.

BY	Suzan-Lori Parks
DIRECTED BY	David Esbjornson
SCENIC DESIGN	Narelle Sissons
COSTUME DESIGN	Elizabeth Hope Clancy
LIGHTING DESIGN	Jane Cox
SOUND DESIGN AND ORIGINAL MUSIC	Donald DiNicola
PRODUCTION DRAMATURG	John Dias
PRODUCTION STAGE MANAGER	Kristen Harris

CAST

HESTER, LA NEGRITA	Charlayne Woodard
JABBER, HER OLDEST CHILD/CHILLI	Rob Campbell

BABY, HER YOUNGEST CHILD/ THE REVEREND D.	Reggie Montgomery
BULLY, HER OLDEST DAUGHTER/ THE WELFARE LADY	Gail Grate
TROUBLE, HER MIDDLE SON/ THE DOCTOR	Bruce MacVittie
BEAUTY, HER YOUNGEST DAUGHTER/ THE AMIGA GRINGA	Deirdre O'Connell

Hester, La Negrita, is the unmarried homeless mother of five children, ages thirteen to two—Jabber, Bully, Trouble, Beauty and Baby. They live under a bridge in a low-rent neighborhood of the city. When the play opens, Hester's oldest son, Jabber, is cleaning the walls of graffiti—the word SLUT—that was painted there by "some bad boys." Hester is still learning to read and write, and the graffiti has soiled her practice place. Jabber, her teacher, claims not to know what the word means. She practices her letters, writing a large "A" on the ground. The other children appear and, after much mayhem, settle down to a meager dinner, then head off to bed. There's no food for Hester.

As she cleans the children's clothing, she is visited by her friend, Amiga Gringa, who has news: Hester's first love, Chilli, is back in town and looking for her. Amiga suggests that Hester contact Baby's father—an urban preacher, Reverend D.—and demand child support.

On her way to the Reverend, Hester is stopped by the Doctor, who examines her. She complains about stomach pains; he gives a little money for food. He suggests she have an operation to remove her "woman's parts"—the fact that she continues to have children despite her poverty frustrates his supervisors.

As she leaves, the Doctor speaks the first of the play's "confessions." In these poetic monologues each of the adult characters reveals and attempts to justify his or her relationship with Hester. The Doctor admits to having used her sexually.

Hester takes a photo of Baby to the Reverend, who refuses to pay but promises to take up a collection in his church—that is, once he builds it.

The Welfare Lady appears for her regular visit with Hester. She is frustrated with Hester and with the children's "deadbeat daddies." She offers Hester an opportunity to make some money—sewing a fancy dress for her wealthy friend. Hester sees Chilli in the distance but doesn't call out to him in order to protect him from the Welfare Lady. Hester takes the clothing fabric and sewing notions.

The Welfare Lady speaks her confession, revealing that she has exploited Hester's vulnerability: to satisfy her husband's sexual desires the Welfare Lady brought Hester to their house for a ménage à trois.

Hester struggles to thread a needle so she can sew the dress. Amiga appears with the news that she is pregnant and plans to sell the baby. She offers to sell the fabric and split the profit so Hester doesn't have to learn to sew. Jabber enters, having wet the bed, looking for comfort from his mother. Bully appears and notices the sandwich Hester bought to quiet her hungry stomach; Hester feeds Bully instead of herself. Trouble enters, sleepwalking; Hester frustrated, sends them all back to bed.

In Amiga's confession, she tells of attempting to manipulate Hester and establish the two of them as lesbian prostitutes and pornographers.

Hester returns to the Reverend to collect the money he promised. He says that his backers have not yet built him his church and that she should return once they have. He cajoles her into performing oral sex.

The Reverend then confesses to having used her sexually—he was turned on by her suffering.

Back at the bridge Chilli visits Hester, dresses her in a wedding gown and proposes marriage. He believes that his son, Jabber, is her only child, and he's proud of the fact that she's managed to make a life all alone. He sings her a love song, "their song." The children appear, and Chilli realizes they are hers. He takes the gown and leaves.

In his confession Chilli admits to having loved her once but sees now that time has changed everything.

Hester takes the children to the backdoor of the Reverend's new church. He tells her that his congregation refused to give money in her name; they are disgusted by her kind. He calls her a slut. She is desperate and destitute. Jabber is scared but tells her that he knows what a slut is and that it was the word that was painted on their graffitied wall. Hester, exploding in a rage, kills Jabber.

Hester is in prison; there is a letter A painted in blood on the floor. Hester confesses no guilt about having had her children and wishes only that she'd had more. The Doctor and the Welfare Lady appear—from a crowd of condemning adults who have surrounded Hester—to confirm that the hysterectomy was a success; she will bear no more children.

Charlayne Woodard (as Hester). Photograph by Michal Daniel.

George Wolfe, producer of the Public Theater in New York City, decides to open the 1999–2000 season with a staging of *In the Blood,* a new play by Suzan-Lori Parks. This will be Suzan-Lori's third production at the Public, but her relationship with George goes back even further. George first met Suzan-Lori in 1990, when he went to BACA Downtown, a theatre in Brooklyn, New York, to see her play, *The Death of the Last Black Man in the Whole Entire World.* She remembers that he said to her then—before he was even hired for his current position—"I'm going to do your plays." Years later he went to New Dramatists for a reading of her *The America Play* and committed to staging it, in a coproduction with the Yale Repertory Theatre, in his first season at the Public (1994). During that production Suzan-Lori was writing *Venus,* and the Public and Yale Rep coproduced this new play the following season (1995).

Suzan-Lori has always earned much praise from academics and literary critics, who appreciate her politically charged poetical riffs on history. They also value her boldly nontraditional, nonlinear storytelling and densely layered dramaturgy, rich with imagery, drunk with language. George Wolfe has said that he admires this about her work but responds strongly to her plays mainly because they are highly theatrical, entertaining and quite moving. It's true that Suzan-Lori's work is challenging to audience members accustomed to the straightforward and traditional. From the very start of her writing career she has broken ground by experimenting with unconventional structures, viewing history through her own lens and combining a wide variety of theatrical and dramatic forms (musical theatre, performance art, stand-up comedy, kitchen-sink realism and the like). Her plays are odd and off-kilter, but at the heart of each is an achingly beautiful, surprisingly funny and horribly honest story of humans in the throes of living. It's these stories that interest Suzan-Lori and engage audiences. She writes plays about characters who are recognizable and often based on figures plucked from history. Suzan-Lori admits to being "obsessed with history." With her plays she attempts to understand events from the past that, when filtered through her imagination, take on a new complexity.

In an essay entitled "Possession," Suzan-Lori wrote:

> Theatre is the place which best allows me to figure out how the world works. What's going on here. So much of the discussion today in literary criticism by Henry Louis Gates, Jr. and the others concerns how the African-American literary contribution should be incorporated into the canon. The history of Literature is in question. And the history of History is in question too. A play is a blueprint of an event: a way of creating and rewriting history through the medium of literature. Since history is a recorded or remembered event, theatre, for me, is the perfect place to "make" history—that is, because so much of African-American history has been unrecorded, disremembered, washed out, one of my tasks as a playwright is to—through literature and the special strange relationship between theatre and real-life—locate the ancestral burial ground, dig for bones, find bones, hear the bones sing, write it down.

Suzan-Lori uses history in her writing not with any reverence for the past nor (God forbid) nostalgia, but rather as a way of showing that the past informs the present and, perhaps more importantly, the present illuminates the past. In her essay "Elements of Style" she wrote that "History is time that won't quit." She also wrote, "Time has a circular shape. Could Time be tricky like the world once was—looking flat from our place on it—and through looking at things beyond the world we found it round? Somehow I think Time could be like this too. Not that I'm planning to write a science book—the goofy idea just helps me NOT to take established shapes for granted. Keeps me awing at it. Attaches the idea Rep & Rev [the name she gives to her technique of repetition and revision of text and events] to a larger shape."

In the Blood is a play about an African-American woman and her five children. As inspiration Suzan-Lori began with Nathaniel Hawthorne's 1850 novel, *The Scarlet Letter,* but the play is not an adaptation of the novel. During rehearsals Suzan-Lori remarked that she couldn't remember when she read the novel, and the details of it mattered much less than what remained of its effect on her. Hawthorne's Hester Prynne—the adulteress heroine of the novel—suffered condemnation by society and manipulation by those close to her. Suzan-Lori recognized the similarity of Hester Prynne's plight to that of a homeless single mother in present-day urban America.

Charlayne Woodard (as Hester) and Rob Campbell (as Chilli). Photograph by Michal Daniel.

Autumn 1998: First reading

Suzan-Lori has continued a friendship and professional relationship with Bonnie Metzgar, who first produced her plays at BACA Downtown and now works as an associate producer at the Public. She asks Bonnie to read *In the Blood* first. Bonnie loves it and brings it to me in the literary department. I read it and am blown away by its daring and maturity. For Producer George Wolfe, the theatre's artistic staff and a few friends we organize a reading for which Suzan-Lori directs and performs (she sings Chilli's song in the second act). It goes beautifully, and George immediately commits to a production for the following season. Most of those present at the reading are quite familiar with Suzan-Lori's work and express amazement at this play, which manages to contain all of the aesthetic wildness and imagination of her prior work within a structure that allows easier access to the story for the audience. Gone is most of the Rep & Rev technique of such earlier plays as *The America Play* and *Venus*. George and the artistic staff (including Bonnie and me) discuss the play and have very few questions and no suggestions for rewrites. We are all eager to see the play tested "on its feet." Since we know Suzan-Lori, we decide there's no need to do further readings or workshops: any problems that might arise with the text are likely be solvable in rehearsal.

The search for a director is simple enough. Suzan-Lori is interested in working with Marcus Stern, who directed *The America Play* at the American Repertory Theatre in Cambridge, Massachusetts. He worked recently at the Public, directing Han Ong's *Chang Fragments*, and George trusts his sense of the theatrical.

Spring and Summer 1999: Preproduction design and casting

Marcus hires an imaginative young scenic designer, Penny Wish, who designed the set for our recent production of *Henry VI*. George's first thoughts are to produce the show in the Public's Shiva Theater—an intimate 105-seat black box. Marcus and Penny have imagined the show in the Public's Anspacher Theater—a 289-seat thrust theatre—a space that George thinks will overwhelm the play despite the intimate relationship of stage to audience. Nonetheless, Penny and Marcus attempt to design a set for the Anspacher. Their design goal is to encourage the audience to feel that they are observing Hester and her family from within their "home" underneath a city bridge. Penny designs a nearly life-size bridge that is to extend from the upstage wall to the back of the house, completely covering one-third of the audience seats. Budget estimates suggest that this set would be very expensive to construct and would mean losing seats in the auditorium. Although the set is visually exciting, George asks them to reconsider and attempt to get the same feeling with a smaller design in the Shiva. After many attempts throughout the summer, and with the contributions of Bonnie Metzgar (as associate producer) and Suzan-Lori, Penny designs a slightly more abstract and smaller bridge for the Shiva. The new design still provides the audience with that same sense of being inside the characters' environment.

Casting the show proves to be equally complex. Marcus generally works with actors who are comfortable within a highly stylized, choreographic staging. He often works in New York with actors from the Off- and Off-Off Broadway theatre who are accustomed to nonrealistic performance styles and nonlinear plays. The Public's casting department and Marcus are looking especially for actors with boldness, daring and a quirky edge, combined with a wide range and the facility for complex language that one expects to find in actors trained to perform the classics. Marcus makes a number of trips to New York (from his home in Boston) for concentrated audition sessions. By early September he finalizes his decisions, and everyone involved feels excited by this very good company of actors.

At the end of the final casting session Marcus walks across the street to have coffee with Casting Director Jordan Thaler; he trips on a broken section of the curb, falls and shatters his kneecap. When he gets home to Boston, he visits a doctor who tells him that he'll need extensive reconstructive surgery, which will keep him off his feet for weeks, possibly months. With rehearsal set to begin in a week, George must make a difficult decision: postpone the production indefinitely and risk sending the season's schedule into tumult, or continue with the production as scheduled with a new director. George decides to postpone the start of rehearsals for two weeks while we attempt to hire a new director and check that the actors will still be available.

David Esbjornson is directing a production of two one-act plays by Maria Irene Fornes at the Signature Theater. Suzan-Lori met David for the first time last year and liked his work. In the previous season at the Public, David directed a successful production of Arthur Miller's *The Ride Down Mount Morgan*. After several meetings and interviews, and with just four days until the start of rehearsal, George hires him to direct the play.

September 27, 1999: Design meeting

The set Penny Wish designed is bold and stark: Its major element is a bridge (possibly painted yellow), which could move somewhat to indicate different locations. Bonnie shows David the model, and he likes it very much but feels that the audience needs to surround the action of the play as much as possible. He wants Penny to redesign the set to accommodate this idea. However, Penny has gone to Europe to work on a project, and she has not planned to be back before mid-October. She will not be able to work on the design with David but is willing to hand over the reins to another designer. The lighting and costume designers hired to work with Marcus also have scheduling conflicts. David decides to hire Elizabeth Hope Clancy, a frequent collaborator, to design costumes, and Jane Cox for the lighting. Bonnie suggests Narelle Sissons, whose work David knows, to design a new set.

Narelle recently worked in the Shiva, designing the set with, director Jo Bonney for last season's production of Diana Son's play, *Stop Kiss.* David and Narelle talk on the phone for a couple of days before arriving at a basic idea for the set, which Narelle then presents for discussion in the form of a model. The Shiva is an intimate space. Its floor plan is rectangular. Its major challenges are posed by the columns that divide the room into quadrants. Narelle's design places the playing space in the long corridor formed by the two rows of columns down the middle of the room. The audience is to be seated in two bleacherlike sections along the opposite lengths of the set.

Production Manager Nick Schwartz-Hall and Technical Director Michael Grant discuss potential difficulties with construction and the task of accommodating an audience within this unusual floor plan. Especially problematic is the issue of sight lines. Jane Cox and Elizabeth Hope Clancy discuss the challenges the set poses to their design elements. Jane worries that containing the light may be difficult within so tight a space and imagines that she'll need to make good use of sharp angles. She and David discuss the possibility of making a virtue of the light spill and consider lighting the audience at certain times (during the "confessions"), to include them in the action. Elizabeth remarks that if the audience is to be so close to the actors the costumes will need to be extremely well detailed, but still simple enough to avoid distracting.

Charlayne Woodard (as Hester), with Gail Grate (as Bully) and Bruce MacVittie (as Trouble). Photograph by Michal Daniel.

Gail Grate, Charlayne Woodard, and Bruce MacVittie. Photograph by Michal Daniel.

Rob Campbell (as Jabber) and Charlayne Woodard (as Hester) in their final confrontation. Photograph by Michal Daniel.

September 28: First rehearsal

Following the Public's official welcoming of the company—the traditional "meet and greet"—the actors assemble around the table with Suzan-Lori, David, the designers, Bonnie and me. Charlayne Woodard is playing Hester, La Negrita; Rob Campbell is Chilli/ Jabber; Gail Grate is The Welfare Lady/Bully; Bruce MacVittie is The Doctor/Trouble; Reggie Montgomery is Reverend D./Baby; and Deirdre O'Connell is The Amiga Gringa/Beauty. We feel fortunate to have this group of actors. David was not, obviously, involved in the casting process, but he knows each of them to varying degrees. Each of the actors has worked at the Public—some many times—and there's a feeling of family. Still I am surprised that with Marcus Stern's sudden departure none of them questioned his or her commitment to the play. Most of them went through a fairly long process of auditioning with Marcus and they surely felt part of Marcus's particular vision of the play. David's work tends to be less highly stylized. His focus is more on the emotional lives of the characters than on the theatricalization. It's a testament to the theatre community's confidence in David and this company's extraordinary range that the actors could easily imagine themselves in two potentially very different productions of this play.

David talks a bit about the visceral and immediate responses he had when he read the script for the first time a week earlier. He says the language of the play sent his head reeling—he felt that he could "hear" the poetry, that it is as alive and honest as anything in Shakespeare—and although the play is wildly imaginative and wickedly artful, he is struck and moved by the immediacy of the story. He has the company proceed with a slow read-through of the play, after which he talks some more about his responses and invites general discussion.

I always love a first read-through. The occasion has that first-day-of-school feeling about it. I also hear the play with a freshness that

allows me to experience it anew. The actors are so raw in their interpretations that the event affords me an opportunity to really grapple with the play's difficulties. I think Suzan-Lori is a little nervous.

I am glad for the questions that came racing to my mind.
There's an economy to every character's speaking style, except the
Reverend. I wonder: will an audience believe he's a big fake if he
goes on too much? Suzan-Lori and I discuss this a bit at the break
and resolve to listen carefully to the progression of his arc, trying
to assess how he's likely to appear to the audience.

I'm fascinated by the "confessions," which are monologues
spaced throughout the play. In these speeches, set apart from the
action of the play, the adult characters reveal and attempt to justify
unsavory aspects of their relationships with Hester. There's a lot to
decipher about them, but I notice their poetic nature. Are they like
songs in a musical? They're written in verse, so the rhythm and line
lengths may give the actors clues (as with Shakespeare) to the
meaning.

We return from break, and David asks Suzan-Lori to tell the
company something of how she came to write the play. Earlier in
the day she told the story to Bonnie Metzgar for an interview to
be published in the program (*Stagebill*). She repeats the story here
for the company: Once when paddling a canoe down a river with
a friend, she made a somewhat flippant comment about wanting
to write a play about *The Scarlet Letter*, which she would call
Fucking A. Then, after making the joke, she started to think about
how the play might actually work; the situation, a story, the characters, all started to come into focus. She says, "I was writing a play
called *Fucking A* as a futuristic version of *The Scarlet Letter*. I was
having a lot of difficulty with it, and about a year ago I got into a
conversation with the characters in the play. To make a long story
short, I decided to change the names of all the characters. The
main character had been called Hester, and I decided to change her
name to something else. I began writing *Fucking A* afresh, and

Hester said, 'What about the play that I'm in?' I listened to what she had to say and let her lead me to a story about a woman with five kids." She eventually worked out all the characters and the complete plot in her head and knew also that each of the adults would have a monologue—a confession—although she had no idea, at that point, what they would say. It wasn't until she sat down at the computer that the confessions "wrote themselves." She calls *In the Blood* her "alien baby" because it emerged from her like the creature from the scientist's chest in the movie, *Alien*. "The play burst out of my chest—boom—the writing process had such a strong and totally terrifying feeling. I wrote a draft, and something wasn't right. Then I realized what it was: the whole play is like a series of woodcuts. The texture of the first draft was wrong; it needed the feeling of a woodcut—very plain and spare—so I wrote the next draft with that feeling in mind."

At the end of the day David and I discuss an issue we are both unsure about. David is getting stuck on the way the letter A is used at the very end of the play. Mirroring one of her first and recurring actions in the play—practicing writing her letters—Hester writes a letter A with the blood of her dead son. In the stage direction, Suzan-Lori has her doing this on the door of a church, which has amassed its own power and meaning for Hester by this point. David and I assume that because the letter is so central to Hawthorne's novel and the novel provided inspiration for the play, this act must have special meaning. Is there, in that action, a desecration of something holy? Is it an act of defiance against the Reverend? Is she reversing the "branding" society has inflicted on her? David is concerned, given the decisions he must soon make about the set, that there might be no actual church door on the stage for Hester to deface.

Fortunately Suzan-Lori joins us at this point in our musings. She tells us, "Hester's just practicing her letters. She happens to be standing next to the church door." Hester is not making any state-

ment, nor is she lashing out against a cruel society. This information gives David permission to approach the play as a story of a
woman's life—the choices she makes and the actions she takes. As
she has often stated, Suzan-Lori isn't looking for anyone to uncover
the metaphoric meaning or the larger societal resonances.

At the end of the day the company all sign a get-well card
for Marcus.

September 29: Second rehearsal

Suzan-Lori comes into rehearsal with some changes she'd like to
make to the first scene between Reverend D. and Hester. Hearing
the play again yesterday, she felt (as I did too) that she'd written
more for him than necessary. It's too early for Reggie Montgomery, who is playing both the Reverend and Baby, to know
what he needs and what he doesn't, so he asks that she keep as
much as possible for a while. David is having difficulty with the
moment in that same scene where the two characters appear to be
in a stalemate. It's in the same area in which Suzan-Lori is both-
ered by the disruption of rhythm. She decides to make a pretty siz-
able cut, removing the pause that confused David and the second
appearance of the Reverend's sermon, which appears on a tape
recording. The actors try it out. Suzan-Lori observes that with a
character such as the Reverend, who speaks so much and, as Hester
says, "built this church just from talking," it's difficult to know, until
you hear it on the stage, how much talking is too much. The cut
seems to be a good one, although Reggie is still unsure. David says
that we have to wait for Reggie to make these rhythms his own
before we can know for certain what's necessary. Suzan-Lori agrees
to hold off looking for more places to trim. David and the actors
continue to work through a cursory discussion of the major shifts
in the action of the story. They get to the end, and Suzan-Lori

Charlayne Woodard (as Hester). Photograph by Michal Daniel.

worries that perhaps the audience won't know that Jabber is killed in one of the final scenes. She hasn't actually written that in the text—none of the characters says anything about it—and she wants to be sure that the audience experiences that important event. We're all pretty confident that the stage image alone will communicate the fact of his death.

David spends the remainder of the rehearsal taking the actors through a discussion of the design elements. He says that, as is always the case, the environment in the Shiva Theater will very much determine and influence the acting style. The set is mostly comprised of a long cement "corridor" or sidewalk that cuts through the middle of the room, bound on both ends by concrete architecture—an arcaded bridge on one end and, at the other, a flat wall with a large metal door in the center. The audience will be in stadium seats along the length, on both sides of the playing area. This relationship to the audience will force the actors to be more presentational, more stylized, at times. And the harsh, cold, unforgiving feeling of the space will affect the way the characters move through and inhabit what is essentially their home. The actors will need to be prepared for the discomfort of living on cement. David wants the audience to be aware of sound on the hard surfaces—the echoes, the rhythm of grit underfoot, the deadness of feet hitting that floor. There's a naturalistic feeling to the set design. It is a real approximation of a hidden urban streetscape, but by its presence in the larger space of the theatre, it becomes quite artful. The design's balance and sense of geometry make the space feel as much imagined as real. David tells the actors, "As much as this may look and feel like places we think we know, this is a *formal* and theatrical space—Greek and classical. Larger than life."

David is hoping that the audience will feel that they are under the bridge with the action of the play. There will be a barrier—a 3-foot wall—between the audience and the playing space, both to help keep actors from being distracted by the close proximity of the audience on both sides and to create an area for the audience, which becomes a metaphorical jury box as events move from the private to the public. He and Sound Designer Donald DiNicola will experiment with subtle amplification of the actors during their confessions, with the hope of making a more intimate connection with the audience and causing the actors to feel more exposed and vulnerable.

Deirdre O'Connell, who plays Beauty and Amiga Gringa, is excited by the challenge of this close relationship with the audience. She suggests that inviting the audience in will help the actors make the audience complicit, allow them to feel a responsibility in Hester's fate. "But," she wonders, "how will anyone expect anything other than a tragic ending?"

This leads to an interesting discussion about the play. Suzan-Lori emphatically states, "Hester is no victim. She is a survivor. But we all need something from her, and she gets under our skin—every one of us. Hester's the one who says, 'My life's my own fault.'"

David says that there is a lot of "mirroring" going on in the play. Each of the characters understands something about himself or herself through Hester's experience. Hester is trying to see herself in the reflection of her children and her lovers. And the audience is forced to see itself as both Hester and her oppressors. David hopes that the fact that the audience is on two sides of the playing space will provide a mirror for the characters within the play— forcing them to reveal themselves, to project their inner selves onto the audience and to receive an image back by way of the audience response—at the same time that it forces the audience to "confront" itself.

David and the designers are grappling with some of the physical demands of the script. Many locales must be represented in quick succession without the benefit of elaborate set changes. David is stumped especially by the need to make the Reverend's church actually appear on the stage.

Suzan-Lori feels that in order for the audience not to dismiss the Reverend as some sort of crazy fraud, there has to be evidence that his backers are real and that he is using the money they give him to erect an actual building. It is true that his ministry is not all that sophisticated—he's been living on the street—but he is making real advances, and what he is doing is legitimate. David is concerned that, because the space is so small and in other ways limiting, whatever it is we see on the stage is bound to look flimsy, undermining the tension of those scenes. He'll talk some more to Narelle.

September 30: Third rehearsal

David asks the company to read through the scenes up to the Doctor's confession. David observes that the play has an astounding forward-moving propulsion to it. The main action—Hester, in crisis, doing what she must to provide for her family—sweeps the audience through her journey. But he's eager to learn how the confessions fit in. Suzan-Lori speaks excitedly about a conversation she and I had in which we tried to graph the action of the play, the way students do in dramatic-literature classes. She says that we can see the play's major action moving in that traditional arc that is slightly upward but mostly horizontal and leads to a climax. But the confessions take the characters (and the audience) vertically—down to deeper truths and revelations. David is intrigued by this notion, and feels the audience can be helped to see the confessions this way if each one comes as a surprise. They must emerge spontaneously from the characters the way they did when Suzan-Lori wrote them—the birth of the alien baby. The audience can react to these surprising forces, thinking, "Oh, so that's what's been going on inside you."

They continue slowly to work through each scene. At the end of the day, Suzan-Lori and I have a conversation about the program. The Public's program for every show—*Stagebill*—is a small magazine with articles about each of the plays currently in production. *Stagebill* Editor Stephanie Coen has planned a lengthy interview between Bonnie Metzgar and Suzan-Lori about the play and about Suzan-Lori's writing in general. In addition, each production is given a couple of pages for the dramaturg's notes. In the past I've written short essays and illustrated them with images—paintings and photographs—that we'd been using in rehearsal. Both Suzan-Lori and I feel that a traditional contextualizing essay will not be helpful to an audience. We don't need to orient the audience toward the sociopolitical world of the play—it's there. And it surrounds us—we are living this every day. We want to let the audience experience the force of the story, to allow them to see the universality of these characters' desires. Suzan-Lori thinks we should perhaps simply reprint the lyrics to Chilli's song. We'll think about it independently.

David and Suzan-Lori continue a conversation about the confessions. They haven't had much time alone, and this seems to me a good, rich topic for discussion. I excuse myself for the day.

October 1: Fourth rehearsal

David tells the company his plan for the next few days' rehearsals: he will schedule a short meeting with each actor to get better acquainted, hash out issues that have arisen and solicit and discuss further thoughts. Beth Clancy will also be around to show and discuss costume sketches. He wants to spend today going slowly through each scene of the play, raising as many questions as possible.

We begin with the prologue that, with the epilogue, represent for Suzan-Lori a theatrical "frame" that contextualizes the other scenes. In both prologue and epilogue a crowd of people surround Hester, scream invectives, sneer, mock and judge her. Like the confessions, the prologue and epilogue force the actors to communicate with the audience in a much more presentational way. Aside from Hester, the characters in the frame are not named. They represent the society at large, which judges Hester. It is Suzan-Lori's intention to have the audience enter and exit the story of the play through the crowd in the prologue/epilogue. The audience will recognize in the crowd, if not their own voices, then voices they hear every day on the street. David says that the prologue is obviously a highly theatrical moment—the writing is very stylized—but that the actors must attempt to create real characters. He wants them to consider the possibility that the lines they speak in the prologue could be spoken by the adult characters they play in the following scenes, as if those characters represent the society at large, which oppresses Hester. Since Suzan-Lori doesn't assign the

Bruce MacVittie (as the Doctor) and Charlayne Woodard (as Hester). Photograph by Michal Daniel.

lines in the prologue, David wants the actors to experiment by taking turns speaking lines and exploring different rhythms and sounds. He gets the entire company to speak in rounds, dividing the actors into groups and parts, assigning lines to certain actors while others simply whisper or something of the sort. While this exercise is a lot of fun, it gets complicated pretty quickly and soon becomes undecipherable; there's so much overlapping of text that we can't make out anything the actors are saying. While David feels very confident about his approach to directing the scenes of the central play, he's less certain about the prologue and epilogue.

I am amazed by Suzan-Lori's ability and eagerness to collaborate "on her feet." She learns from the actors and contributes to their discoveries. In a number of interchanges with David and the actors she has made many quick, precise, smart changes to the text.

Moving on to the first scene, Rob Campbell (who is cast as both the child Jabber and the adult Chilli) has a question about playing the children. Rob is wondering if each child is intended to be a small version of the adult played by the same actor. David suggests that this question would be a good place to start. We all begin to notice relationships within some of the pairings: Jabber is Chilli's son; Jabber is Hester's favorite, but she kills him; Chilli is her true love, but he destroys her. Reverend is Baby's father; Reverend is the most articulate; Baby doesn't speak. Bully is aggressive; Welfare Lady is passive. Beauty is vain; Amiga Gringa is self-obsessed. Later Reggie asks if they are actually playing children or merely being inhabited by the essence of a child. Again David suggests that they resist playing an essence or an idea but rather search for the details and variations that make these real people. The actors occasionally raise questions about the lives of homeless people or the realities of life on the street. They take inspiration from some of the photographs the designers have been using for research. After rehearsal Suzan-Lori, David and I discuss whether I should bring in additional research. David does not want to give the production a specific sociological or political message. The gut-wrenching gravity of the situation must be seen as real and possible, but the play's impact on an audience—its universality—will surely come from its heightened and expansive artfulness. And so far the actors seem to be having no trouble connecting to the reality as they search for the style.

In the evening I leave for a five-day trip to Los Angeles to see a few shows for the Public.

October 6: Second week of rehearsal

David begins to stage the play today. While I was away, David's discussions with the actors prompted him to propose to Suzan-Lori some cuts and changes to a number of the scenes. I regret that I wasn't around. The changes mainly try to clarify the storytelling in the scenes between Hester and the Reverend. I question making these changes so early in the process—before any attempts to stage the scenes are made. I trust David but believe that he will discover the play more "on his feet" than if he had been hired earlier, and he needs to give himself time to do this. We also want to be sure that the company is being challenged by the complexities of the play and that they are not looking for problems to be simply "cleared away." I consider how this is always the goal when rehearsing a new play, but I just worry a bit that we are under special circumstances because of David's recent arrival. I realize my reaction may be a function of my absence—not having been a part of the discovery—mixed with some degree of guilt and regret.

On a break Suzan-Lori and I again discuss the dramaturgy pages for the program. Still concerned about the clues we give the audience as to how to watch the play, I suggest that we find some text from *The Scarlet Letter* that will evoke the themes of the play. We both remember a passage early in the book about the letter "A."

Suzan-Lori is not convinced and wants to go away to consider the idea. Later that evening she leaves a message on my voice mail. She'd been reading through the novel and found the following passage, which she wants to print in the program:

> Wisely judging that one token of her shame would but poorly serve to hide another, she took the baby on her arm, and, with a burning blush, and yet a haughty smile, and a glance that would not be abashed, looked around at her townspeople and neighbors. On the breast of her gown, in fine red cloth, surrounded with an elaborate embroidery and fantastic flourishes of gold-thread, appeared the letter A. It was so artistically done, and with so much fertility and gorgeous luxuriance of fancy that it had all the effect of a last and fitting decoration to the apparel which she wore.

In order to underline a central idea of the play—that the "branding" of Hester doesn't fully separate her from the people around her—we decide also to reprint the following passage:

> She felt or fancied, then, that the scarlet letter had endowed her with a new sense. She shuddered to believe, yet could not help believing, that it gave her a sympathetic knowledge of the hidden sin in other hearts. She was terror-stricken by the revelations that were thus made. What were they? That the outward guise of purity was but a lie, and that, if truth were everywhere to be shown, a scarlet letter would blaze forth on many a bosom besides Hester Prynne's?

> —From *The Scarlet Letter*, Nathaniel Hawthorne

October 9

During this week David spends most of the time with the actors on their feet. He asks lots of questions that enable the actors to locate the emotional and psychological realities of the characters. They struggle to find, in their physical demeanors, details to indicate situation without becoming too much like a documentary.

Early on, they grapple with Suzan-Lori's performance instructions included in the body of the play and signaled chiefly by page lay-out. These are instructions for what Suzan-Lori calls "spells" and "rests." For example, the entire company is working on the following section in the first scene:

The children burst into tears.

HESTER

Cmmeer. Cmmeer. Mama loves you. Shes just tired is all. Lemmie hug you.

They nestle around her and she hugs them.

HESTER

My 5 treasures. My 5 joys.

HESTER

JABBER/BULLY/TROUBLE/BEAUTY/BABY

HESTER

HESTER

Lets hit the sack! And leave yr shoes for polish and yr shirts and blouses for press. You dont wanna look like you dont got nobody.

They take off their shoes and tops and go inside leaving Hester outside alone.

HESTER

HESTER

HESTER

(Rest)

*She examines the empty soup pot, shines the kids' shoes, "presses"
their clothes.*

HESTER

You didn't eat, Hester. And the pain in yr gut comes from
having nothing in it.
(Rest)
Kids ate good though. Ate their soup all up. They wont starve.
(Rest)

Suzan-Lori indicates that a character has a "spell" by printing the
character's name as a speech heading without spoken dialogue following. In the preceding example the first spell is Hester's, followed
by a spell shared among the five children, then returning to another
spell for Hester. David explains that during a spell the character is
locked in mid-action. She must be *poised,* without taking a *pause;*
she may appear to the audience to have stopped her action (moving or speaking), but the energy and rhythm of the action must
continue to be felt by the actors on stage. It may appear that she is
hanging up the action for the others in the scene, unless, as in the
example, the others are also in a spell. He suggests that a motiva-
tion for a spell, if thought through by the character, might be
something like, "I can't afford to go down the path I'm heading,
so I must negotiate with those around me where I'll go next." But
there is no break, no pause in the *underlying* action or rhythm.
Suzan-Lori is attuned to the rhythms of each character's speech,
thought and actions and (much as in the verse of Shakespeare) she
indicates the continuations, variations and stops of those rhythms.
Charlayne's experiments have led her to try using the spells as an

Reggie Montgomery (as Reverend D.) and Charlayne Woodard (as Hester).
Photograph by Michal Daniel.

opportunity to lock eyes with a scene partner and "speak the subtext with a look." David encourages her, and asks that all the actors
try holding the moments of a spell for as long as possible to experience all that is possible in them. The "rests," they discover, function more as traditional pauses in the action and rhythm. Charlayne
is perplexed, in the above section, by the three successive spells she
has alone. As she attempts to use them to connect the action of her
previous line with that of her succeeding line, she sees how they
help to keep the forward motion going by easing the transition
from the rhythm of one line and action to the rhythm of the next.

October 12

David spends a good deal of time with Charlayne and Reggie
working on the Act I scenes between Hester and Reverend D.
With Suzan-Lori present, they make great strides identifying the
structure of their evolving relationship. Suzan-Lori begins to realize that some of the moments between these two characters go on
too long and take the momentum out of the building tension.
With the help of the actors she now sees that the events are stacked
too heavily in the first scene, and she decides to move one entire
section to a later scene.

October 13

Today's focus is the relationship between Hester and the Doctor.
Bruce MacVittie (who plays the Doctor and Trouble) is the first
actor to take a shot at staging a confession. Suzan-Lori wants each
confession to be announced. David wants to experiment with a
few approaches. He asks Bruce to speak the text titled: "First
Confession: The Doctor; Times Are Tough: What Can We Do?"

as the Doctor, as another character in the play, as a disembodied voice and, in a metatheatrical way, as Bruce the actor. Each strategy has its merits, but it's still too early to know how the confessions need to function. David goes back to working on the scene between Hester and the Doctor, hoping to see how that action leads to the confession.

October 15

David works with Gail Grate (who plays the Welfare Lady and Bully) and Charlayne for most of the day. Working on the scene between the Welfare Lady and Hester, Suzan-Lori finds some small internal cuts. She is hearing little repetitions that she doesn't like or doesn't need now. She also is beginning to see that some of her stage directions are unnecessary. For instance, at one point in the scene Suzan-Lori has written that the Welfare Lady "pops" Hester. Given what Gail is doing with her voice and physical attitude, Suzan-Lori decides that the Welfare Lady no longer actually needs to hit Hester.

October 16

I watch David and Deirdre working on Amiga Gringa's confession. David asks her to try it as a conversation with the audience. This device allows her to use the space more freely. Although she has memorized the text, she stops quite often and is easily distracted. She realizes that the relationship with the audience is making her feel more exposed, more vulnerable. Suzan-Lori thinks there may be elements of that sensation that are appropriate—making these confessions *should* be uncomfortable for the characters. They must not use the confessions as an opportunity to charm the audience.

This work with Deirdre helps David to find some new approaches to the confessions. They continue to be the most elusive elements to him. They are some of the more theatrical (and nonrealistic) moments in the play. The confessions and the prologue/epilogue provide the greatest opportunity for theatrical interpretation. Since David has been pushing as hard as he can just to get through the scene work, he's concerned that he has given short shrift to these more theatrical moments.

October 17–18

The company stumbles through the first, then the second act. David is concerned that he hasn't figured out the sweep and force of the final two scenes of the play. He knows that much depends upon the pace and rhythm of Charlayne's work during the emotional climax of the play. Suzan-Lori feels that the actors peak emotionally too early in the play and that there seems to be more than one dramatic climax. David recognizes that he and the company have been most interested in shaping the relationships between and the actions involving Hester and the adults who apply the pressure to drive her through the play. As a result of this concentrated exploration, the events that drive Hester to her final act are all very clearly felt. After seeing the stumble-through, David realizes that he needs to spend more time with the actors sculpting moments in scenes with the children. The actors have not yet created children the audience can imagine surviving this lifestyle; as it is now, they seem doomed from the very start. David wants the actors to find a way for the audience to invest in the children. The audience should care about their future without anticipating the ending from the very start.

October 22

A run-through is scheduled. David has just returned from a whirl-wind trip that took him out of town for a couple days—one of the commitments that, given the last-minute nature of his hiring, he was unable to relinquish. This has meant that he's had no time to address all the observations we made in the stumble-throughs. In attendance: George Wolfe, Bonnie Metzgar and the designers. David is eager for a run-through but frustrated for the actors and worried that George and Bonnie will see only what he *hasn't* done. The running time is much longer than we expected, the result of very slow pacing by the actors and an overly long first act. I try to imagine how Charlayne will manage this performance every night. She is on stage almost every minute, and it's a rough ride for poor old Hester—both the emotional and the physical ups and downs are intense. But Charlayne appears to have infinite energy resources. Everyone in attendance is clearly moved by her bravery, valor and generosity. Already there's a level of honesty—an atten-tion to the detail and truthfulness of every moment—that we rarely see, even in a fully rehearsed show. This is a testament to David's focus and the fine collaboration he's had with the actors. But there's clearly an imbalance at this point—a heaviness that is too much for both the actors and the audience. Suzan-Lori, David, Bonnie and I meet later in the day with George in his office.

George's notes for David are mostly observations having to do with problems of pacing. He feels that there needs to be a more overall sculpting of Hester's emotional and dramatic (active) arcs throughout the play. So much obviously depends on getting it right in the first scene. George observes that Hester "has a 'stupid' heart, which has forced her to learn all kinds of survival skills to compensate and protect herself." He appreciates the richness that David has helped the actors to discover but thinks that Charlayne needs to find more emotional economy and to drive through all her actions, especially in that first scene. The first scene begins in medias res, and we must feel that we are catching Hester in a daily routine and that she is, at least at home, in command. She must be actively participating in these moments, and the audience should feel the sweep of events. She cannot become reflective in the midst of the action but only when she's alone, and then at the very end. Emotional analysis slows down the action. George realizes that the actors are still in a process of discovery—the emotional lives of the characters are valid and "true" for where they are right now—but he thinks David ought to jump-start them into "more action than emotion." I think David had a very similar insight before he went away on that trip. He is frustrated because he has not had time to address this "imbalance."

George also asks a number of questions about the nature of the confessions: What is the literal event of each one—what is the character actually doing? What is the character's relationship to the audience? Is the character under some pressure to speak? We're all feeling that the confessions are not punctuating the characters' journeys nor contributing sufficiently to Hester's forward arc.

October 26–31: Technical rehearsals

Flu season has apparently started early this year, and the virus is beginning to make its way around the company. A couple of actors have been showing up late, and everyone is looking a little bleary-eyed.

There are no major problems with any of the technical elements, and each day the company is on or ahead of schedule. The design elements are simple enough and the sound and light cues are being written rather quickly. As a result David uses the extra time with the actors to shape their performances. He fills in detail in the scenes with the children and makes great strides. The more David and the actors work to create those distinct characters, the more real they become—even in rehearsal. I remark that rehearsals often feel as if we are missing half the cast. There are eleven distinct characters, but because of double-casting, there are only ever six actors in the room.

The set looks much as Narelle had presented it in the model. The floor is comprised of the concrete slabs used to make city sidewalks. The linear pattern of the floor is beautifully broken by a skewed slab, which is raised somewhat over a top corner of another as if a shift in the earth below had caused the sidewalk to buckle. It looks great and adds considerably to the gritty naturalism. The Reverend's church will not actually appear on stage, which relieves the crew of potential difficulties. Instead it will be represented by one of the doors in the arcade of the bridge. The lighting helps the space to feel enclosed. The light catches the actors at sharp angles and in broken patterns, as if light from above is being impeded by overhead structures. The costumes are tasteful and sometimes ironic—Beauty's dress has a classic silhouette but looks more silly than beautiful; Bully's eyeglasses are big and obvious and make her look nerdy rather than threatening. There's certainly a feeling that the clothes are found objects and not deliberate, but they're not ugly, dirty or torn. They project hope and a sense that someone takes care of them.

Suzan-Lori also uses this smooth tech period to explore some changes. In our notes meetings following the run-throughs, we all feel that the rhythm of the first part of Act I was off—that there seem to be too many events. Suzan-Lori and I notice two obvious cuts that, we think, might help the pace and rhythm. There's part of a scene in which the conversation between Amiga and Hester is interrupted by three separate appearances by the children. There are good reasons, contributing both to the dramatic action and character definition, for each appearance, but we could save a good deal of stage time and keep things moving if we cut Trouble's "sleepwalking" entrance. The second idea for a cut is in the following scene between Hester and the Doctor. In that scene

Gail Grate (bottom; as the Welfare Lady) visiting Hester at home. Photograph by Michal Daniel.

the Doctor is performing a street-side physical exam—a theatrical interpretation of the random and careless health care given to people on the street. I think Suzan-Lori imagined the exam taking place much more quickly than is actually possible, and it is now quite easy for her to see places to trim. We are loath to try implementing both of these fairly major cuts together. Both involve the same actor—Bruce—who plays Trouble and the Doctor, and we don't want him thinking that he's doing something wrong. David also believes that the Trouble sleepwalking moment may be important enough allow for a glitch in the rhythm. David and Suzan-Lori work out some cuts to both the text and the blocking of the Doctor's exam. Bruce and Assistant Director Nora Francescani rehearse the new scene in another room for a while before Suzan-Lori and I join them. Bruce is naturally having some difficulty attaching new lines to old blocking and vice versa. Susan-Lori and I suggest additional ways to simplify.

In a phone conversation one evening Suzan-Lori and I discuss the "reunion" scene between Chilli and Hester late in Act II. Something about the way the tension builds seems not quite right. Suzan-Lori is frustrated that she cannot find an answer. We're reaching that point in tech where everyone's tired.

The next morning Suzan-Lori comes to rehearsal with new excitement and a solution. After our phone conversation she watched a videotape of Rodgers and Hammerstein's *The Sound of Music* and was inspired. When she first tells me, I think she's joking. But she explains, and it is a great idea. The scene in the film where the young lovers sing "Sixteen Going on Seventeen" takes place in a romantic gazebo. The girl sings with excitement and anticipation, looking innocent and hopeful in her beautiful dress. That sense of hopefulness, which in the end is smashed, is what Suzan-Lori is trying to build in the reunion scene. We realize that Hester needs to wear the wedding dress sooner, so that we can see her living in a moment of hope before Chilli rips it away from her.

The actors try out the shift of lines and blocking; the scene is now perfect and heartbreaking.

Bonnie and I are still concerned with the uncertainties about the confessions and the problem of the languorous rhythm of the first scene. We decide to push David toward addressing these problems before previews. Over the course of a difficult dinner meeting we realize that he can't see solutions until he sees the whole of the production in front of an audience. We all recognize additionally that until the prologue is staged satisfactorily, we'll never properly gauge the rhythm of the first scene. The prologue should give us a way into the play (and that problematic first scene), and at this stage in David's exploration we're unclear what it tells the audience.

Because of the close proximity of the audience to the stage, lighting alone cannot hide the fact that the actors in the prologue/epilogue—the frame—are the same actors as in the rest of the play. David is determined that the audience must not think that the children are speaking as members of the crowd in those framing scenes. There's no opportunity to change the costumes between the prologue and the first scene. Stark, angular lighting keeps the actors mainly in shadow during the prologue, and Beth Clancy attempts to hide actors' identities with dark overcoats. David tries a number of staging and cueing techniques to heighten the theatricality of the frame.

November 1

At the final dress rehearsal George, Bonnie and others from the theatre's staff join the production team as audience. Many of the earlier issues reemerge, along with a new one: We're all feeling a strange hiccup, a sense of abruptness, at the end of Act I. We're not sure why but hope that the reaction of an audience will help enlighten us.

November 2: First preview

In rehearsal today Suzan-Lori asks the actors to drop certain text throughout the play. In some instances it's just a line or two she wants to cut—mainly to keep things clipping along. She and David have been feeling for some time that there needs to be a substantial cut to Amiga Gringa's first speech about the economic realities of life on the street. It's a long-winded, funny rant. Much of its humor comes from its length—it's full of embellishment and over-dramatization. The problem is keeping the action, which exists underneath all this language, clear. The sheer volume of words is getting in Deirdre's way, and despite her valiant efforts the audience loses track of her objective in the scene. This is a painful cut for Suzan-Lori to make. I think Deirdre's not happy either—the laughs are fun to get, and she's clearly an extraordinary actor, who doesn't give up easily.

One of the great things about the configuration of the playing area and its intimacy is that from wherever I sit, I have a clear view of both the action on stage and the faces of half the audience. Admittedly, I am more interested in the audience than the actors tonight, and feel that audience members are reasonably engaged throughout. I notice them losing interest at certain points and not laughing in all the "right" places, but finding more humor than I expected. They seem to accept the confessions uncritically. I think they're willing to allow the confessing character more forgiveness than Suzan-Lori intends. They are also stumped by the prologue, and especially the epilogue. I think the audience experiences the epilogue only as an afterthought to Hester's final and powerful confession.

The flu virus that's been traveling through the cast and crew hits David with a wallop. He has a difficult time focusing during the postshow notes session with George. George has a number of questions about Hester's relationship to the Reverend. The dramatic movement of Hester through the play is very much dependent on the increasing tension of the scenes with the Reverend. The hope of salvation through him is what begins and ends her journey. George feels that tension must be tightened—felt more palpably. He suggests that Suzan-Lori trim some of the scenes in which the Reverend is alone onstage and instead put him in contact with Hester more often. We all have ideas for cuts and rearrangements that should help to that end.

George also identifies the problem with the hiccup at the end of Act I and has a great idea for a solution. He notices that the audience leaves for intermission having just heard the Welfare Lady's confession and having witnessed a small, awkward moment when Hester's children come to be by her side. He suggests that the audience needs to leave the act with the focus very strongly on Hester. We should see her on the precipice of the next part of her journey, which takes us into Act II. His idea is that after the Welfare Lady's confession Hester should see Chilli again and call after him. Early in the act there's an anticipation and sense of hope when Amiga tells Hester that Chilli's back in town and looking for her. The audience needs a restatement of that hope before the intermission. Everyone loves this idea. Naturally it has consequences that Suzan-Lori and I attempt to address before making the change in the next day's rehearsal. Mainly she needs to make some textual changes later in the act.

Everyone feels that there is an inevitability that takes over in the final quarter of the play. The action spins out of control, then must come to an end and resolve itself without lingering. The epilogue seems to be getting in the way. David proposes combining the final scene and the epilogue into one final movement. He suggests to Suzan-Lori some of the ways in which this might work, and she responds with some additional possibilities. However, cutting the epilogue clearly disrupts Suzan-Lori's idea of framing the play. She still feels that without it she won't accomplish what she set out to do with the play—to land it all back in the audience's lap. She'll sleep on it tonight.

November 3–15: Previews

Casting Directors Jordan Thaler and Heidi Griffiths attend an early preview, which is the first performance that seems not to succeed with the audience. The actors are working so hard that they reach an emotional pitch during the show that's difficult to modulate.

Suzan-Lori decides to make the change to the epilogue and final scene. In the latter the Welfare Lady and the Doctor discuss the success of Hester's hysterectomy while in prison. As originally written, the epilogue follows that scene and is basically a repetition of the prologue. Now Suzan-Lori decides to combine the two scenes by embedding a shortened version of the Doctor/Welfare Lady scene within the epilogue. The idea of an epilogue still exists, and the event seems to complement the prologue, but it is now a part of the dramatic action that ends with Hester's downfall. I like the way the rhythm of the final few moments is speeded up. The audience doesn't have time to reflect on the events of the final few scenes while they're happening; now there's a series of shocks, without time to recover, until the end. It has been a tough change for the actors to integrate in just one rehearsal. The lines of the epilogue are staccato non sequiturs—difficult for the actors to learn and more difficult to rearrange. In the cutting and reworking, Suzan-Lori sacrifices some of her prerogative to keep what she wants in order to make it easier for the actors. Still, they stumble through it tonight.

Heading home, Jordan and I share a cab; his reactions to the show are insightful and helpful. He loved it and felt that the audience was completely enthralled. I realize that I've been watching too often; I'm losing perspective. I ask what he thinks of the frame.

He is reminded of *Fellini's Casanova,* which I have never seen. What he remembers most clearly of the film are its opening and closing moments. It begins with a crowd of peasants running through the streets of an eighteenth century village, chasing and then mauling an elegantly dressed aristocratic man. The action happens very quickly, and the audience doesn't know the characters or situation but Jordan felt sympathy for the man. The next scene begins the story of Casanova's life. The movie ends exactly as it began—with that fast chase through the village streets. What Jordan found so striking about the film was "seeing" the beginning at the end, when he understood finally the situation and characters. Now he sympathized with the peasants and cheered them on. I love this notion (and want now to see the film), and we discuss its relationship to the play. To have the initial frame repeat itself exactly at the end, something must happen to the audience's perception, based on what it watched in the intervening scenes. When I get home, I call Suzan-Lori and we try using the example of the *Casanova* frame to track through our audiences' changing perceptions of Hester. The next day in rehearsal Suzan-Lori and David hash out ideas about the prologue. Neither is satisfied yet.

After seeing a few preview performances, Bonnie and I are still the most vocal about the need to address two outstanding issues: the rhythm problems in the first scene and the literal nature of the confessions. I'm still advocating that we try to cut the "Trouble sleepwalking" bit, and David is the most resistant. I still believe it's the key to solving the problem of the dragging rhythm in the first half of Act I. The scene is full of wonderful detail—of both character and situation—but I feel that it keeps the audience from the action for too long. We all agree that there is a problem with rhythm; David feels that it can be solved with faster pacing of the scene.

Bonnie is concerned that David be given plenty of time to rethink completely the approach to the confessions. We do not

Hester with the dressmaking materials from the Welfare Lady. Photograph by Michal Daniel.

have the luxury of full rehearsal days, and David tries to work out ideas in note sessions with George and the creative team before going to the actors. The adjustments that he is making to the confessions are not changing much. The basic conception remains the same: The lights fill the stage and the house, and the actors speak the confessions directly to the audience. Bonnie suggests that they be made more theatrical and less naturalistic—that the audience be drawn in, rather than spoken to directly.

Between Saturday night's performance and the Sunday matinee David and Suzan-Lori work out a plan to cut the prologue completely. With the epilogue now functioning as part of the dramatic action and incorporating the final preepilogue scene, the plan of a mirroring frame for the play is already corrupted. David proposes that cutting the frame would be a clean solution to the problem of figuring out the meaning of the prologue/epilogue repetition. It's a radical decision, but it doesn't drastically affect the actors or the cues for the stage managers. The cut goes in on Sunday without rehearsal. Unbelievably, the first scene moves like gangbusters. The play begins now in a very dangerous place—very much in the middle of a vulnerable moment for Hester. It's a brilliant stroke, of either genius or luck. I think this change shakes up the actors as much as it does the scene and causes them to move at a quicker pace. And without the prologue the first half of the act doesn't seem as long and the rhythms have all changed. I'm beginning to think we should keep the "sleepwalking" beat. This reshaping of Suzan-Lori's vision of the arc of the entire event is serious. Suzan-Lori is worried about the absence of a device that would have called into question the audience's sense of responsibility. But she recognizes the value of an active collaboration with a director, actors, dramaturg, producers and audience. She knows that each change and cut makes this production work more successfully but that in another production it might work differently. In her mind she will "bracket" the cut of the frame. She needs to live with it for a while. (A month after the show closes, she tells me that she's decided to make permanent these changes to the beginning and ending of the play. The shocking and simple start to the play arrests the audience in the way she always intended for the prologue.)

Thursday night George comes to the show, and we meet in his office afterward for notes. We're getting close to opening and will need to freeze the show soon. David has only a few more days to rehearse. Among his notes George has three primary issues to address.

First, he feels that the first scene still goes on too long and he advocates for the "sleepwalking" cut. David plans to tighten the moment by increasing the actors' pacing.

Second, he feels that the confessions do not drive the play

forward—they seem to provide both the actors and the audience with an unnecessary rest. George and David get into a heated, exciting discussion of the confessions, and I see that they're making headway. George manages to communicate his feeling that the characters delivering the confessions are given too much space—literally and figuratively. He moves animatedly around the room to prove that we listen less carefully when he is moving about. When he remains still and is confined to a small space, we pay more attention to his words and to his internal struggle.

Third, George finds that the solution we all worked out for the end of Act I doesn't go far enough—that there needs to be still more focus on Hester. Suzan-Lori and I had been feeling as George does about the end of Act I, and we search the middle of the play for a way to solve the problem. We suggest moving the top of Scene 1 in Act II (which is almost continuous in time with the end of Act I) to the end of the Welfare Lady's confession. The Welfare Lady will exit after her confession, leaving Hester alone onstage to begin sewing the cloth the Welfare Lady left her. Hester will experience a pain in her gut, double over and recover, to see Chilli in the distance. This way there will be more time for the scene to shift from one that is primarily about the Welfare Lady to a private moment with Hester. Suzan-Lori must return to those changes she made previously in the act to address Chilli's new entrance.

Over the next few days' rehearsal David puts in the change to the end of Act I and a few small cuts to Act I; Scene 1. He does manage to tighten the pacing, which helps the problem of rhythm. He also makes radical changes to the staging of all the confessions. Jane Cox hangs some new lights, so that each confession can be confined to a different, small, delineated square of light on the stage. This lighting forces the character into a kind of hot seat, with the audience as judge and jury. The impression now is of characters trying to justify their actions rather than solicit sympathy from the audience. It is a hugely successful change. There is a sharper focus now on the complicity of Hester's friends and acquaintances in her tragedy.

November 22: Opening night

Bonnie and I spend the day together shopping for opening-night gifts. We've both felt very close to this production and invested a good deal of ourselves in it. I appreciate this opportunity to buy presents and ritualize the project's completion. Opening night goes well, but it's not the best show the actors have performed. Fortunately most of the critics were at last week's performances, which were more consistently good shows.

I think about Suzan-Lori's vigilant attention to her vision and David's care and respect for it, and all the work of everyone who loved this play. If everyone who sees this play leaves the theatre with the experience Margo Jefferson describes, then perhaps we have accomplished something:

> Parks and Hawthorne share an obsession with American history and the larger patterns of sin, cruelty, punishment, and redemption that give it form and content. *In the Blood* is about the way we live now, and it is truly harrowing. We cannot turn away, and we do not want to. You will leave feeling pity and terror. And because it is a work of art, you will leave thrilled, ever comforted by its mastery.
>
> —Margo Jefferson,
> "*The Scarlet Letter*, Alive and Bitter in the Inner City." *New York Times*, November 23, 1999.

John Dias is an Associate Producer at the The Joseph Papp Public Theater/New York Shakespeare Festival where he has worked since 1994. Before coming to New York, he was the Literary Manager/Dramaturg at Hartford Stage Company in Connecticut, and since then he has worked as a dramaturg with a number of playwrights and directors. He has consulted for the National Endowment for the Arts, the Connecticut Commission for the Arts, the New York State Council for the Arts and the Drama League. He teaches Shakespeare's text to actors in the Public Theater/NYSF Shakespeare Lab.

BIBLIOGRAPHY

Hawthorne, Nathaniel. *The Scarlet Letter.* Boston: Houghton Mifflin, 1929.

Jefferson, Margo. "*The Scarlet Letter,* Alive and Bitter in the Inner City." *New York Times,* November 23, 1999.

Parks, Suzan-Lori. "Alien Baby." Interview by Bonnie Metzgar. *Stagebill,* December 1999, p. 50–58.

———. "Elements of Style." In *The America Play and Other Works.* New York: Theatre Communications Group, 1995.

———. "Possession." In *The America Play and Other Works.* New York: Theatre Communications Group, 1995.

Savran, David. *The Playwright's Voice: American Dramatists on Memory, Writing and the Politics of Culture.* New York: Theatre Communications Group, 1999.

Solomon, Alisa. "Signifying on the Signifyin': The Plays of Suzan-Lori Parks." *Theater,* Vol. 21, No. 3, 1990.

$\mathcal{G}$EOGRAPHY

AT YALE REPERTORY THEATRE

by Katherine Profeta

In October 1997, the Yale Repertory Theatre premiered *Geography*, a new work of theatre and dance conceived and directed by the postmodern dancer-choreographer, Ralph Lemon. In collaboration with the American poet, Tracie Morris; one other American dancer; and seven traditional dancers and drummers from Guinea and Côte d'Ivoire, Lemon set out to explore his racial, cultural and artistic identity. Beginning without a preexisting script, Lemon built his production chiefly from cross-cultural and interpersonal experiences and discoveries made within the rehearsal hall. Katherine Profeta, who created this notebook, was a dramaturgy student at the Yale School of Drama during her work on *Geography*. She returned to Yale after graduation to work with Lemon on *Tree: Part 2 of The Geography Trilogy*, which premiered in the spring of 2000.

CONCEIVED, CHOREOGRAPHED AND DIRECTED BY	Ralph Lemon
TEXT	Tracie Morris
SOUND SCORES	Francisco López, Paul D. Miller, a.k.a. DJ Spooky That Subliminal Kid
SENSORS	Paul D. Miller, a.k.a. DJ Spooky That Subliminal Kid; realized with Ralph Lemon
VISUAL ART	Nari Ward
COSTUME DESIGN	Liz Prince
LIGHTING DESIGN	Stan Pressner

SOUND DESIGN	Rob Gorton
PRODUCTION DRAMATURGY	Peter Novak,
	Katherine Profeta
STAGE MANAGEMENT	Jenny Friend
ENGLISH/FRENCH INTERPRETATION	Orida Boukhezer-Diabaté

CAST

FROM GUINEA/U.S.	Djeli Moussa Diabaté
FROM GROUPE KI–YI–M'BOCK CÔTE D'IVOIRE	Djédjé Djédjé, Nai Zou, Goulei Tchépoho, Zaoli Mabo Tapé
FROM ENSEMBLE KOTEBA CÔTE D'IVOIRE	Akpa Yves Didier ("James"), Kouakou Yao ("Angelo")
FROM U.S.	Carlos Funn, Ralph Lemon
LIVE PERCUSSIVE MUSIC	Djeli Moussa Diabaté, Goulei Tchépoho, Zaoli Mabo Tapé, Carlos Funn

PERFORMANCE ORDER OF MAJOR ELEMENTS
YALE REPERTORY THEATRE OPENING NIGHT
(ADAPTED FROM THE STAGE MANAGER'S SHIFT PLOT)

	Approximate Performance Time *Min.: Sec.*
MAP	
The Prologue (Tapé and Goulei)	1:30
CRIME	
Map Poem (Originally Called "Intro/Outro")	2:32
Pygmy Dance	2:00
Moussa Solo	3:37
Path Phrase Duet with "Mene Mene"	3:23
Circle Dance with Satellites	4:40
Collage/Quartet/Drum Quartet	10:18
"Overview"	6:42
TRIAL	
Large Minuet Circle	1:38
Tire Talk	1:50
Minuet Square	1:15
Minuet	3:40
Rock Throwing	1:35
Haiku	0:30
Purification	5:00

DIVINATION

Singing on Ladders/Bottle Curtains	2:25
Haikus	2:10
Angelo, Ralph, Moussa Trio	2:30
Divination Dance	5:59
Tapé and Goulei Drum Duet	2:05
Moussa and Angelo Duet	0:34
Endurance (James and Djédjé)	7:52
Ralph and Carlos Duet	1:00
Moussa Solo Text	Not Specified

A month into my first year as a dramaturgy student at the Yale School of Drama, I heard that a mysterious, experimental dance work was being planned for the following year's Yale Repertory Theatre season. It would be directed and choreographed by Ralph Lemon, it would involve African dancers, it would be titled *Geography* —and that's all anyone would say. I put my bid in early for the position of dramaturg, brazenly insisting that it was a perfect job for me, without knowing any more details about the project. I thought involving myself in this piece would be the ideal way for me to integrate my lifelong love of dance and my new career as a dramaturg. What's more, most of the dancers would come from Francophone West Africa, and I could speak French.

At the same time Peter Novak, another dramaturgy student at the school, was putting in his bid. He had a particular interest in postcolonial studies, and predicted that the themes of *Geography* would fall along these lines. He also had experience as a speech and voice coach and would be able to help nonactors learn to speak text on stage. In the end Peter and I didn't need to compete—the faculty decided we would serve as co-dramaturgs. Because our strengths were so different and complementary, it would be easy for us to share the job. I would stay a little closer to Ralph Lemon, the director/choreographer, and Peter would stay a little closer to Tracie Morris, the poet who was slated to write the text.

In *Volume I* of *The Production Notebooks* Christopher Baker, who chronicled Robert Wilson's *Danton's Death*, asks, "How does one go about dramaturging a dance?" Perhaps this notebook will help answer his question. My experience as a choreographer came in handy; the ability to talk about movement both mechanically and thematically was particularly helpful. But mainly I considered my responsibility to be threefold, just as it is on any dramaturgy project I undertake: research, synthesis and questioning. I was to research new avenues of investigation, help synthesize what was going on in the rehearsal room through my observations and ask lots of questions (most pertinent, some impertinent) along the way. These actions apply equally well to dance, theatre and realms in between.

I think the broader question that my experience on *Geography* may help to answer is: how does one dramaturg a piece of "devised theatre" (as the British call it)? In other words, how does one serve as a dramaturg for a work that begins without a preexisting script and will be developed entirely from experiments within the rehearsal room? In any project built from scratch there's a fine line between artistic freedom and artistic free fall. The only person who can decide when it's best to keep options open and when they should be limited, the only person who can say whether a given note is perfectly crucial or perfectly irrelevant, is the one at the center of the storm, the director/choreographer. Work on this type of production can be frustrating for a dramaturg. The terms of the production remain in flux an uncomfortably long time, and it's much harder to look into the future and anticipate what will be needed a week or even a day ahead. On the other hand nothing beats the thrill of discovering moments that are richer and more organically linked to the performers than anything one could have planned in advance—and devised theatre relies entirely on such discoveries. The dramaturg's role in fostering these discoveries is potentially more creative, more participatory and, ultimately, I think, more rewarding.

March 1996

Ralph Lemon catches a train from New York to New Haven. Two great supporters of American dance, Sam Miller and Cynthia Mayeda, have set up a meeting for him and Stan Wojewodski, Jr., the artistic director of Yale Repertory Theatre. On the train Ralph takes out a piece of paper and writes down what he might want to do, given the chance to create a piece at Yale.

The meeting is opportune because both Ralph and Stan have reason to be interested in the possibilities the other offers. In October 1995 Ralph presented his dance company's final concert before disbanding the group. He decided to release himself from the traditional model of choreographer-with-a-company and explore other models for creating work. Stan, for his part, is interested in throwing a wild card into his solidly drama-based season. In an earlier meeting Stan, Sam, Cynthia and Mark Bly (Yale's associate artistic director) had discussed the possibility of producing dance within the resident theatre structure. Stan wants to nurture a thoroughly experimental project—perhaps something that combines dance and theatre?

Ralph sketches out an idea based on collaboration with traditional dancers from Haiti and West Africa. He's already been to Haiti, last November, in conjunction with the documentary film collage he's making on the Haitian community in Miami. And he has an embryonic plan to go to the Côte d'Ivoire (also known as the Ivory Coast) in the near future, to visit new contacts there. The idea of working with Haitian and West African dancers is full of

personal, emotional challenges, and at this moment Ralph is looking for ways to challenge himself. The issues are not only private
but public: in the past critics took him to task for having an all-
white dance company, implying that he was "betraying his race."
What's more, some went so far as to intimate that his highly formal, abstract choreography was an inherently "white" art form.
Ralph will defend to the bitter end his right to be a black formal-
ist, but he *is* curious about undertaking a personal exploration of
race and cultural identity at this turning point in his career. He also
hopes that the Haitian and West African dancers, whose contexts
for dancing are so different from his own, will help him forge a
new relationship to the stage.

The meeting goes very well. Stan asks Ralph to continue
developing his ideas. Ralph returns to New York and begins working up a more specific plan of action with the help of Ann
Rosenthal, the head of Multi-Arts Projects and Productions
(MAPP), the management company working for him since his
dance company disbanded.

June 1996

Stan, Victoria Nolan (Yale Rep's managing director), Mark,
Catherine Sheehy (Yale Rep's resident dramaturg), Sam, Cynthia,
Ann and Ralph all meet in New York. They are joined by Mikki
Shepard, the director of 651, An Arts Center in Brooklyn. Mikki
is on board now to help support the workshop phases of the pro-
ject through 651's Africa Exchange program. And as 651 shares the
Majestic Theater with the Brooklyn Academy of Music (BAM),
she will try to present the final project in conjunction with BAM's
Next Wave Festival.

Much time is spent talking through the longer developmental time frame of the dance world, as opposed to the resident the-

Ralph Lemon behind Nari Ward's bedspring curtain. Photograph by T. Charles Erickson.

atre world. Stan first pushes for a presentation at Yale next spring, as the final slot in the 1996–97 season. Ralph and Ann, secretly afraid that they are being offered that slot or nothing at all, nervously explain why it would be impossible to execute such a project in less than a year. To their relief Stan switches tack and offers them the first slot in the 1997–98 season. In that way the entire summer of 1997 will be open for workshops, before the official four-week rehearsal period begins at Yale in the fall. Yale will also support a workshop period in the late spring of 1997.

A defining moment occurs when Ralph mentions needing support for his trip to Africa and Stan quickly responds with an offer of money from his discretionary fund, reserved for Associate Artists of the Yale Repertory Theatre. From that moment onward Ann and Ralph know that Yale is fully committed. After the meeting they continue developing more and more specific timelines, and Ann starts writing grant applications in conjunction with Victoria Nolan.

August 1996

Ralph goes to West Africa—to the Côte d'Ivoire and Ghana—looking for musicians and dancers he can invite to collaborate. He sticks to the cities, having decided that for the purposes of this project he needs to work with performers from urban areas. He would also prefer to work with performers who are used to the routine of a dance company. In this way the cultural differences between Ralph and his collaborators, unavoidably large as they will be, can at least be mitigated by some analogous experience.

The most promising contacts are with Souleymane Koly and WereWere Liking, artistic directors of two well-known dance and theatre companies in Abidjan, Côte d'Ivoire—the Ensemble Koteba and Groupe Ki-Yi M'Bock. Ralph watches both groups rehearse and perform. Lacking a context in the world of African dance, he finds it hard to know on what grounds to evaluate the dancers—in his journal he writes: "I think that all that I can judge is anatomic alertness." He creates a list of performers in whom he saw this alertness and to whom he felt a more immediate connection. Upon his return to the United States he corresponds regularly with the two directors in Abidjan, trying to arrange for the performers' participation.

Fall 1996

Grants begin coming through, and Ralph begins to locate his other collaborators—designers, composers, a poet. He invites Carlos Funn, a young African-American dancer he met while teaching at Virginia Commonwealth University, to be the only other American performer on stage. And he asks Djeli Moussa Diabaté ("Moussa"), a Guinean man who lives in Brooklyn and is descended from a long line of griots, to join as well. (A griot is responsible for knowing the songs, dances, history and mythology of his people and occupies a revered position in West African culture). Meanwhile, Ann books a United States tour that will take *Geography* to Minnesota, Texas and North Carolina following the Yale premiere.

The relationship between MAPP and Yale is more firmly established. MAPP is a small company used to working closely with its artists and their last-minute needs; Yale Rep is a large organization with an extensive permanent support staff working on many projects all at once. It is decided that MAPP will officially produce *Geography* in exchange for a fee and Yale will officially serve as the project's first presenter, but in actuality the producing burden will be more evenly shared according to the strengths of the two different organizations.

Slowly, throughout the fall, the possibility of working with the

Haitian artists becomes more and more remote. Regular communication is difficult because of some personal crises on the other end, and the necessary momentum is never generated. By the end of November it becomes clear that the Haitians won't be participating.

Spring 1997

In March Ralph takes a second trip to Africa to see the Ivoirean performers again and to solidify the arrangements that have been taking shape.

In early May I meet Ralph for the first time. We share a quick conversation and some comments on how exciting the work is sure to be. I think he is a little dubious about the idea of working with a dramaturg, much less two. But even if we had many advance conversations, I doubt it would be clear how best to prepare for the workshop. Ralph's one specific request is that I keep a notebook of daily observations on the collaborative process, focusing particularly on issues of cultural exchange.

May 27, 1997: First day of the preliminary workshop

The cast arrives: Ralph and Moussa from New York, Carlos Funn from Virginia, and the rest touching down at JFK Airport from far-off Abidjan, van-driven the last lap to New Haven. I go to this morning's meet-and-greet in the lobby of the University Theatre. The folks who gather to greet the new arrivals include the Yale Rep support staff, interested Drama School students, and most of the members of Ralph's production team. The Africans are immediately distinguishable from the African-Americans in the room: they have a subtly different carriage, a different way of taking up space. This impression is, however, exaggerated by the fact that the entire roomful of people has fallen into intersecting orbits, all revolving around our foreign guests.

The cast assembles inside the theatre. The dancers and drummers, each by now outfitted with a "Hello My Name Is" badge, sit with Ralph on the edge of the stage, feet dangling. The rest of us sit in the house. We go down the line with introductions. First there is Moussa, a wiry, authoritative Guinean man who lives the expatriate life in Brooklyn. His wife, Orida Boukhezer-Diabaté, has signed on to be the interpreter for the project; she's an Algerian woman who grew up in Paris. Moussa's children are also along: the two little girls, Bijou and Fatou, are well behaved as they sit in the audience. They look to be about 5 and 2 years old respectively.

Next Djédjé Djédjé introduces himself, taking care to mention that he, the dancer next to him, and the two drummers at the other end of the stage are all members of Ki-Yi M'Bock, a pan-African performance group with a spiritual focus. Djédjé wears a complete formal African ensemble, at one extreme in a clothing continuum that ranges from mostly-Western to traditional African. He possesses a tone of authority similar to Moussa's, and has a cool remove about him. Next is Nai Zou, Djédjé's fellow dancer, the largest man there, with powerful features but an incongruously gentle voice. Kouakou Yao ("Angelo") and Akpa Yves Didier ("James") sit next to Nai. The two of them belong to the other respected Abidjan dance company, the Ensemble Koteba, and there is a slight hint of competitive pride in the way they introduce this fact. Angelo is angular and energetic, and (at the other end of the clothing continuum) he sports stylish Western garb. James is tall, broad-faced but otherwise thin as a rail. A single cowrie shell hangs importantly, like a third eye, in the middle of his forehead. After Angelo and James come Goulei Tchépoho and Zaoli Mabo Tapé ("Tapé"), the drummers and least senior members of the group. Tapé is a young man of very few words, introducing himself abruptly, definitively, quickly. Goulei takes a little longer, as he's more polite and soft-spoken than Tapé. That's it for the Africans, but further down the stage's edge sits Carlos Funn, the young African-American dancer from Virginia. He introduces himself briefly, the first who doesn't need Orida's interpretive aid to talk to the audience (Orida now turns to translate his words for the others). Carlos has a hint of that laid-back southern attitude in his speech and his manner. He also seems to be holding himself back, keeping to the side, just taking it all in.

After the other collaborators and the New Haven staff have identified themselves, Moussa gathers the cast together into a circle in front of the stage. He wants to say a prayer before beginning rehearsals, so that all may begin properly, with open hearts. As the circle assembles, a few others go up to join: Stan, Tracie Morris (the poet), Jenny Friend (our stage manager). Gradually more and more folks from the audience deem it appropriate to join as well, until the once-modest circle is forced to move up onto the stage, now wide enough to fill the entire playing area. I'm up there too, one of many holding hands and listening, eyes closed, as first Moussa and then Djédjé direct our thoughts out over the month to come and deliver their prayers for a successful workshop.

After this invocation most of the observers leave, and a smaller group assembles onstage. Ralph summarizes his inspirations for *Geography*, evoking the African diaspora and his own upbringing as an African-American firmly ensconced within the European-American tradition. "I have looked at African culture from a great distance," he confesses. Up until now. He compares the two dance traditions: "The European style of dance is more formal, more mechanical . . . it dances the spirit out of the body. I don't find this bad, but it is what I've inherited." For Ralph, these West African dancers promise not just new ways of moving but also new perspectives on *why* one dances. He tells them that he's interested in hearing their ideas about their own dancing. He knows that their dancing has a greater spiritual component than his does. Then he

Djédjé Djédjé and Akpa Yves Didier ("James") in front of the curtain of suspended glass bottles. Photograph by T. Charles Erickson.

warns them that although this will be a collaboration, he is ultimately the choreographer for the project, and he will be directing their experiments. He hopes these experiments will lead to new forms, to new ideas about what kind of dancing they are all capable of. His assumptions about dancing will hit up against their own, and the clash, if all goes well, will be a productive one. Yet he doesn't want to exploit, or do anything improper to their work. He needs to know how open they are to experimentation, how willing to try strange hybrid ideas.

I have been waiting to see how Ralph would broach this question and what the response will be. The dancers should all be aware of Ralph's general concept for the collaboration, and yet most of Ralph's negotiations in Africa were, for reasons of cultural decorum, undertaken with the artistic directors of the two dance companies rather than the dancers themselves. Djédjé is the first to respond. He defines African dance as consisting of three circles: a secular circle, where everyone may dance; a circle where only initiates may dance (he implies that all the dancers here have attained that level); and a third circle, making use of masks and ritual objects, which is the most sacred of all. This third circle, where the dancer is closest to the gods, is off limits for a project such as Ralph is describing, but the other two may easily be used. Everyone in the room seems content with this analysis—there are clear boundaries, and some things will remain sacred, but on the near side of those boundaries an exciting experiment will take place.

Ralph next addresses his thoughts about music and rhythm. Though he deeply respects traditional African drumming, he doesn't want to make use of this music without putting it through the same process of experimentation. The idea is to find new forms that combine their interests and his own. Ralph is intrigued by rhythmic breaks and discontinuities; he doesn't like incessant, long-standing repetition. Perhaps the drummers can find ways to experiment with discontinuity; he invites them to be creative. By way of example he takes out a small handheld tape recorder and hits "Play." We hear a tinny recording of an African drum solo in which the rhythm is slippery, elusive, continually shifting. It turns out that the recording is a result of work Moussa and Ralph have already done together in New York. Tapé and Goulei nod, not willing to say more at this early stage.

Carlos, who still sits slightly apart, becomes the focus of attention as Ralph explains how he imagines his role in all this. Since Carlos has studied African dance (with the legendary Chuck Davis, down in Virginia) and also knows Ralph's contemporary American style, he will offer Ralph a reference point in both traditions. What Orida is doing for the spoken word Carlos will help do for the movement. What's more, Carlos is also fluent in house (a form of club dancing that blends different social dancing styles, African-based dance styles and martial arts) and *capoeira* (a dancelike Brazilian martial art). Both house and *capoeira* embody a strong African influence as translated across the Atlantic. Thus Carlos will not just facilitate the process of exchange, his presence will also compound the levels of translation taking place in this room.

Ralph describes the absent collaborators and their roles. Nari Ward is a New York sculptor of Jamaican descent, and his custom-made installations will serve as our scenery. This will be his first time working on a formal stage production. Nari's work usually consists of huge assemblages of urban detritus, wherein old materials are woven, burned, riveted, torn, sewn, glued and thereby transformed into something new. Ralph imagines that Nari's scenic installation will evoke both contemporary urban America and contemporary urban Africa—the real, everyday habitats of every artist in this room. Liz Prince, the costume designer, is a white woman from New York with years of experience designing for dance. As a result of her discussions with Ralph she is already planning two costumes for each dancer: one business suit and one flowing white gown.

Contrary to my expectations, the Africans show no resistance to this last idea. There's not even much surprise. Djédjé simply asks, "Why will we be dressed in gowns, are we supposed to play women?" Ralph replies, "No, you are not dressed as women or acting like women, you are simply men wearing gowns. It's our attempt to soften the male physique. It's also an attempt to acknowledge the fact that there are no women on stage, to make a point of that absence." Someone else quickly inquires, "Why did you choose only male dancers?" Ralph replies simply, "Because this is an autobiographical work." He uses the word "autobiography" loosely, to indicate that *Geography* will necessarily extend from his own history and point of view. As a black male artist collaborating with other black male artists, he intends to explore and challenge his racial and cultural roots, his spirituality, his reasons for dancing—all elements of his self-understanding.

Tracie Morris takes her turn to speak. She's an African-American poet—Brooklyn born and raised, with all the no-bull-shit attitude that hometown implies, and her small-boned frame belies the large force of her personality. She's won many performance awards with her poetry at venues such as the Nyorican Poet's Café and National Poetry Slams. As her poems are meant to be spoken aloud, they operate through musical values as much as through textual ones. She tells us that she's interested in helping the audience gain access to the piece through the concrete value of words, but, at the same time she likes to create her own music and rhythm through the abstract sound value of language.

Tracie has a great personal interest in exploring the links between African and African-American culture. She has studied the subject considerably. Ralph comes to the *Geography* project essentially brand-new, preferring to stay away from too many general historical conclusions in order to react solely to what's in front of him, but Tracie wants to work with everything she already knows. She tells us that she aims to get beyond the easy stereotypes that Africans and African-Americans have of each other, to the real essence of their similarities and differences. And she brings up something she observed earlier: when Carlos introduced the fact that he studied African dance with Chuck Davis, Moussa reacted in a way that seemed dismissive. This is an example of how the two groups might stereotype each other, and she finds moments like this very interesting. Moments like this become her subject matter.

I too had noticed the moment Tracie refers to—after Carlos mentioned Chuck Davis, Moussa had said something to the other Africans, in a French too fast for me to decipher, and mimed some hand gestures that might have been mocking. I wasn't sure. Now Moussa takes great pains to explain himself, saying no, he wasn't being negative about Chuck Davis, he'd only been telling the others who Davis is: an African-American who gets a lot of money from the United Sates government to research and perform African dance. This is our first moment of explicit cultural tension, catalyzed purposefully by Tracie. For a moment the air in the room is taut, but the incident blows over quickly, spirited away by an abundance of good will on both sides. What just happened? Tracie was acting bold by bringing possible conflict to the fore because she wants to use it as her subject instead of glossing over it. Indeed, every little incident that takes place in this rehearsal hall becomes potential subject matter, and that's why I find myself with a notebook on my lap, keeping detailed notes on all that comes to pass. And yet, as I write in that same notebook: "We must make sure to put ourselves (the Americans) on the spot too."

Tracie and Ralph move on to describe how Aeschylus' *Oresteia* will serve as a narrative backbone for the piece. They summarize the story briefly. Ralph finds a productive tension between this classic story of European civilization and all the black bodies performing on stage. The story will be interpreted loosely, but it will lend structure to the piece and a general progression toward redemption. Orestes is in exile from his homeland, and when he returns it is both to commit murder and to find peace. Ralph and Tracie imply a deep connection between the African-American experience and Orestes' narrative journey.

I haven't heard this described so explicitly before and I wonder how the violence in the story is going to be interpreted, both by our African collaborators and by our eventual audience. Djédjé is on top of this question immediately:

DJÉDJÉ: Why this man, and what does he have against people? He returns to kill his mother?
RALPH: We're making an analogy to the real and potential destruction that exists between African-American and African cultures.
TRACIE: Note that I think something is *wrong* with Orestes. I don't accept his position. There is something wrong with him *because* of his exile.

We leave it at that, for now. At the end of the day the biggest of the many hanging question marks concerns this use of *The Oresteia*. At the moment I don't think any of the Africans understand why they're being asked to help tell this story. Neither does Ralph, really—he just knows he wants to use it as a point of entry. But if you graft the idea of Orestes as an exile on to the position of African-Americans as exiles, you get the story of a return in which an African-American goes back to Africa to destroy his roots. Is that the story Ralph wants to tell? I don't think so, but I'm not sure I know what he wants instead. I do know that there is a lot of violence lurking in his inspirational imagery, violence that I don't yet understand.

The other major question is articulated by Nai. After listening to Ralph speak eloquently but abstractly about the collaboration, Nai raises his hand and asks point-blank: "On what basis shall we work? Are we going into your style? Or you into ours?" Ralph explains that, with only three months of combined workshop and rehearsal time, there won't be enough time to work out all possible methods of exchange. That given, he intends to bring the dancers into his world, yet in a way that remains respectful of their own. In so doing, his own world will be changed, his assumptions questioned. Ralph asks us all for our trust and patience because, as he puts it, he won't know where he's going until right before he gets there.

May 28–31

This first week has been rich. Everyone in the cast is drop-dead talented, and Ralph is a seemingly endless source of avenues for investigation. I've never been so eager to go sit in a rehearsal room. I feel like I'm dancing, vicariously, when in truth I'm just sitting on my butt penciling page after page of notes.

   I do join the dancers for the first event of every day, which is a yoga warm-up led by Ralph, with either Orida or me interpreting. Yoga is familiar to Ralph and Carlos, mostly or completely strange to the Africans. Extreme flexibility isn't a priority in African dance the way it is in contemporary American dance. Thus the morning yoga ritual is a time for intense concentration as the dancers throw themselves into a completely new technique. But it's also a good time for cracking jokes: on Ralph's valiant but flawed attempts to speak French, on what our different bodies can and cannot do, on the culture shock the Africans are currently experiencing.

   After yoga, Tapé and Goulei start in with the drums, and the dancers solo in their own styles. Djédjé is the best at remaining completely unflappable, riding coolly above the most heated steps. With Angelo it's all about sharpness and speed: his feet are a blur as they blast through their staccato patterns. And James, with his long limbs, seems to fly like a bird that is gangly on the ground and suddenly elegant in the air. Ralph, when it is his turn, dances to

Ralph Lemon behind the bedspring curtain. Photograph by T. Charles Erickson.

the African drums in his own loose, shifting, individual style, but I see hints of the quick feet of those who went before him. After the first day Ralph makes specific requests before each improvisational session: he asks to see the most complex footwork they know, or he asks them to repeat themselves as little as possible. The improv sessions are videotaped for later reference.

On the third day Ralph introduces a new form of improvisation. Dancers work in pairs and learn to support each other's body weight in a flowing, spontaneous exchange. Ralph demonstrates how relaxed the body should be by picking up five-year-old Bijou and swinging her loose body in great arcs. "Perfect!" he declares, as she giggles explosively. The dancers throw themselves into this new task, exploring, and soon they are flying off each other's bodies, leaning and lifting and occasionally crashing to the ground.

We continue the exercises for a couple of days. James soon notices the links between these improvisations and Ralph's own movement style. When prompted, he demonstrates by doing a keen imitation of Ralph dancing and explaining that he finds the same loose-bodied feeling whenever he gives over his weight to another dancer. His comment leads to a long discussion about African dance versus "Ralph's style," which the dancers find slow by comparison. Moussa makes the point that in African dance the drums are so hot that they warm you and push you to go fast—there's almost no choice in the matter! In Ralph's style, he contrasts, you just "let yourself go." The music doesn't push you or warm you.

THE PATH PHRASE AND THE PIGMY PHRASE

On the first day Ralph taught everyone a phrase of his own devising but wasn't satisfied with the result. Because they were expending too much effort to look like him, they weren't using their own strengths as dancers. The burning question for Ralph is how to push the boundaries of what the Africans can do without asking them to do something completely awkward and alien. The next day Ralph comes in with an answer: he will observe the dancers' steps and rhythms, loosely translate them into his own style and then teach that translation back to them. The result is a double translation: the Africans' version of Ralph's version of African steps. Ralph is now calling this material the Path Phrase, because he has initiated a path toward the Africans so that they may find a path toward him.

Carlos, James and Moussa take the responsibility for learning this material. James has an immediate affinity for Ralph's style. The way he moves on his own already has certain similarities to Ralph's, and so he's doing amazing work, though he's a perfectionist and keeps pausing to criticize himself harshly. Moussa is having a more awkward time of it, as the different sections of his body want to stay isolated, and he misses Ralph's particular way of finding echoing connections between body parts (what American dancers call "sequencing"). Neither James nor Moussa looks quite like Ralph while dancing these steps—and that's not the point. But in James the tension between styles is productive, while in Moussa it's borderline frustrating. To Carlos, of course, Ralph's style is familiar, and he helps James and Moussa work through it all.

On the third day Ralph sits down with Djédjé in front of a video of Djédjé improvising. He chooses a section where Djédjé is playing with a particularly quirky step, subtler than most, with small limb accents and a wobbly head. Using the remote control, Ralph starts and stops the tape, indicating a number of discreet passages to be reproduced perfectly and pasted together into a new phrase. Ralph isolates the least regular and most off-balance passages and then asks Djédjé to connect them without any internal repetition. The loss of repetition is particularly tricky, as often in African dance a step executed to the right is followed by the same step to the left, and the dancer's body comes to expect that symmetry. But Djédjé, after a few hours with the remote control in hand, masters the assignment. The resulting phrase is even quirkier than the original as it continually shifts and surprises the observer. Angelo and Nai learn it from Djédjé in one day, although they don't quite capture the style that he brings to it. Angelo has as much difficulty trying to capture Djédjé's style as Moussa is having across the stage with Ralph's style—a welcome check to the idea that African versus American is the only stylistic distinction worth making.

Ralph asks Djédjé's group to perform the new phrase while wearing the rehearsal suits (all collected from New Haven second-hand shops, but elegant nevertheless in dark blues, browns and charcoal grays). The effect is remarkable. An African dance step performed in a conservative, Western power suit obviously creates a feeling of incongruity. But just as strong is the uncanny congruity between the cool subtlety of this particular step and the cool, *GQ* attitude the dancers take on while wearing these clothes. We feel an opposition, but it also makes perfect sense. To my American eyes this is a new way for a black man to be empowered in a suit: not power through conformity, but power through redefinition.

We sit to discuss, and Ralph asks how it feels to be doing this dance in suits. Nai suggests that it makes an interesting *mélange* (mixture), because the source step is from the Pygmy culture, in the middle of the African forest. Pygmies wear only loincloths, he adds. So if you know that, it's interesting to see it done in Western suits, and it creates something new. Ralph asks Djédjé, "From where do you know this dance?" Djédjé replies that the Ki-Yi company was doing research on Pygmies and they learned the dance off television, from a documentary about Pygmy culture. Minutes later, during a break, Ralph exclaims to me, "What a perfect shattering of my expectations! I think he's going to answer, 'In the bush,' and instead he says, 'On TV'!"

On the first day of the workshop I noticed myself falling into the assumption that the Africans were here to represent tradition and Ralph and Carlos were here to represent innovation. But again and again this week I've seen how much the tension between innovation and tradition is already present in contemporary West African culture. The Ivoireans all come from the midst of urban Abidjan, where the culture is alive, moving and redefining itself. Where an urban setting and pan-African ideals mean that life is full of cultural exchanges and mixtures. Where people argue about old ways versus new ways, and the compromises that are made are uniquely African compromises. Ralph seeks to engage contemporary West African culture, so the African "tradition" he's interested in is not the one that's fixed in the Western imagination but the one that continues to evolve.

June 4

I'm still wondering exactly how we will develop our connection to *The Oresteia*. Both Peter Novak and I reread it, and we walk around all day with dog-eared copies under our arms, but we aren't quite sure how to apply the information to the work occurring in the rehearsal room. This much, at least, has become clear: Ralph has divided Orestes' saga into four parts, as he sees it: Map (Agamemnon), Crime (The Libation Bearers), Trial (The Eumenides) and Divination (The Eumenides). This interpretive step is the given from which we will begin, and these four sections will give us the shape of the work.

Ralph and I sit down to chat after rehearsal. Settling into the red plush seats of the auditorium, and gesturing toward a stage that had been full of activity a half-hour before, I ask him about the violent imagery behind *Geography*. If what we're staging is a return to homeland and roots, and if Ralph-as-Orestes makes his return in order to commit a violent crime, how will that crime be represented? What will the audience see? Ralph's images have been so fluid that I am unsure of how specific a reference he wants to make. But I am sure that the audience, understanding this piece as a collaboration between Africans and African-Americans, will try very hard to understand the implications of any violent imagery. I ask Ralph: does he want these images to be specifically politicized? If so, is it United States-on-Africa violence or is it rather as if the

American presence catalyzes intra-African violence? Is Ralph-as-Orestes always the perpetrator or is he sometimes the victim as well? Will the audience see an easily legible source for the bloody images, will it have a sense of cause and effect?

Ralph replies that he is thinking of violence as a simple fact of existence more than anything else—violence predates Orestes' return from exile and will continue after him. The cycle of violence doesn't end even with the Eumenides. So we're not meant to focus on Orestes' return as a catalyst for violence, which is the interpretative leap I'd been making until now. For Ralph violence is cyclical, it erupts and dies down periodically, without clear cause. Its potential is part of the simple reality of everyday life for a black man, whether in the United States or in Africa. It is this general sensation, rather than a narrative of cause and effect, that he hopes to convey.

The word "responsibility" keeps cropping up as we talk about how the violence in the piece will be perceived. We easily agree that the point is not to feed into existing stereotypes linking African-American men and violence. I speculate that few audience members would be simplistic enough to take the violence onstage as an essentialist statement about black men. But I do think that our audience will read this piece in its postcolonial context and try to read the violence as a statement about violence within Africa (of which there is plenty to be had in certain countries, but not the countries from which our dancers come) or about the violence inherent in the clash between African and European-based cultures or even about a subtler kind of potential violence in meetings between Africans and African-Americans—the violence of finding misunderstandings where one expects brotherhood. But what exactly the audience will see, and how explicitly it will beg these sorts of interpretations, I don't know.

At this point my questions can only be anticipatory and speculative. Ralph, for his part, is reluctant to pin things down so soon in what should be an exploratory workshop. But he is intrigued by the fact that I'm sensitized to issues of violence and wonders if this is somehow related to my point of view as a woman or, more specifically, as a white woman. I say no, I don't think so, but of course it's impossible for me to really answer. We laugh at that impossibility. Ralph finishes by reiterating that his goal for *Geography* is to pose interesting questions and explore difficulties. He's more interested in meeting that goal than in conveying one clear statement on the relations between African and African-American men.

June 5

"INTRO/OUTRO" AND "OVERVIEW"

Tracie brings in poems inspired by *The Oresteia* and the idea of African/African-American collaboration. From a number of options Ralph selects two with which to begin: "Intro/Outro," a sound poem for one voice, and "Overview," a conversation for two voices. "Intro/Outro" will be performed by Ralph at the top of the show. At the end of rehearsals Ralph often stays late with Tracie and Peter (who has considerable experience as a speech coach) to work on his vocal performance. He repeats a single word—first "womb," then "more," then "room"—over and over until it dissolves into pure sound and intermittently pops back into meaning. The "Intro" portion ends with the repetition of the word "map." Ralph spits out this word with staccato urgency—is it a declaration, or a request? The "Outro" section, which immediately follows, repeats the phrases "this garden," "is scarred," "is guarded" and then, finally, "is dead." It hints of a lost Eden, a missing home.

In "Overview," two exiled characters try to describe their world, where nothing sits quite right:

```
in this
in this heaven
in this heaven
like
hell


we affirm an inverted                    invented
God


it is either a void          to avoid
  or blinding light                       blinding
either way i see nought                   drought
but blue                     blues
```

The second voice serves as a punning, contentious echo to the first. The text is dense and allusive, and the two disagreeing voices purposefully complicate our understanding of the world they describe. Tracie rehearses "Overview," with Ralph and Carlos playing the first and second voices respectively.

Tracie, Ralph, Peter and I discuss different ways to include the African performers in the textual work. Tracie feels strongly that whatever is said on stage should have importance for everyone in the cast. We all agree. But what approach is best? Ralph has an idea: we translate the first portion of "Overview" into French, hand out Xerox copies, and then ask the Africans to translate that French into their West African languages—Bete, Baule, Susu, Malinke and Guerre. Ralph experiments with different ways of staging the dancers while they speak their translations. But after a day and a half of work this idea gets shelved. The dancers don't seem to be connecting to the poem on a personal level—it's not a style of poetry with which they're familiar. What's more, the process of translating and explaining the poem is unreasonably time-consuming.

Tracie changes tack and begins holding individual rehearsals with Moussa and Djédjé when either one can be spared from dance rehearsals. They go off to find a private space in the lobby or a classroom, often with Peter accompanying them. Her intent is to write poems tailored specifically to their voices and their points of view.

June 1–7

THE COLLAGE PHRASE

Ralph's choreographic experiments bear much fruit over the second week of work. On Monday he announces that he's going to review the videos of the dancers improvising and pull out sections of movement from each, pasting the pieces together into one large phrase which we will call, appropriately enough, the Collage Phrase. He works with the dancers one by one over several days, extracting and condensing their material, with the goal of preserving just those moments which are most interesting to his eye. This is the same process he employed with the Pygmy Dance, but now multiplied across six different dancers and even more different kinds of dances. He begins with Moussa, instructing him to take nine separate passages and attach them end to end without repetition. Moussa finds it particularly hard to pull his steps out of context and thwart the expectation that a gesture on the right side will be followed by the same gesture on the left. Ralph observes: "It's as if I've cut off half his body, just by asking him not to repeat!"

Soon Moussa, having just barely put the sequence together, is asked to teach it to the others, while Ralph pulls Nai out of the group to begin constructing the next sequence. This process continues until every dancer has helped form one section of a larger phrase, which everyone will learn. Ralph insists that each dancer's personal style be preserved within the section he originated. But because each dancer's section is almost as strange to him as to the others, constructed as it is from different passages of his movement pasted together, much deliberation is required to decide exactly how to execute a section and keep it within an understandable rhythm.

Translation breaks down as the Africans get into intricate discussions on the fine points of steps and musicality. Often by the time Orida has succeeded in translating the subject of a discussion, the dancers have resolved that point and are on to the next complicated issue, or the one after that. So Ralph, having caused the maelstrom with his brazen requests, gladly steps back and lets it play itself out. Carlos also stops giving input, sitting down and waiting for the final outcome of any given deliberation. The Africans remain at the center of the storm, completely absorbed in their task.

The drummers join the fray—they have just as many opinions as the dancers on how a step should properly be danced, especially on how it should mesh with the rhythm they're playing. Their role in these deliberations highlights the different relation between musician and dancer in African culture: while the contemporary American dancer generally expects the music to remain constant and the dancing to either meet or not meet the music based on the dancer's will, the Africans expect musician and dancer to collaborate and meet in the middle. It is as much the drummer's responsibility to match the dancer's steps as it is the dancer's responsibility to stay with the music. Thus a good African drummer is not only a good musician; he also has a keen eye for movement. We discover this fact repeatedly as either Tapé or Goulei steps forward and offers the resolution to a particularly tricky dilemma.

Now that the work is absorbing everyone's attention, the room is livelier and personalities are less inhibited. Angelo begins yelling, "Ah, so!" whenever he likes another dancer's contribution. At first I am confused by this, thinking it some kind of faux-Japanese joke, but later discover he's actually saying: "Asso!"—short for *mon associé* (my partner, my pal). Soon everyone in the room, Ralph included, is yelling "Asso!" Another African phrase becomes popular as well: "Molo Molo Kai," which is used to mean "take it slowly." Carlos quickly latches on to this phrase, as he is perpetually in need of someone to show him a step several notches slower than the usual African tempo. (Later Nai explains to me that "Molo Molo Kai" is actually the name of a particular dance from Zaire, one that proceeds more slowly than the majority of African dances.)

Now Ralph extends the Collage Phrase by choreographing in front of the whole group, in the moment, instead of turning back to the video. He describes the kind of step he's imagining and asks for contributions. He wants something with involved foot-work. Or he wants something that contrasts with the previous rhythm. The dancers propose different solutions, from which he picks his favorite. Ralph also collages in several passages from his own style, and the African rhythm is temporarily broken while his looser, slower energy takes over.

THE QUARTET PHRASE

A new section emerges, which we call the Quartet Phrase, since it involves only the four Ivoirean dancers. Moussa and Carlos are still working to master the Collage Phrase, but the Ivoireans are eager to move forward, so Ralph continues with just four. And he ups the ante. Taking a newly created passage, he divides it in half, call-ing the first portion A and the second portion B. He then asks two dancers to dance AB and two dancers to dance BA, noting that if all works out correctly, the four should finish at the same time. But this result is more elusive than expected, primarily because the drummers' rhythm must work equally well for both parts. We try it over and over, but the dancers never finish exactly together. There's always an irksome *décalage* (slippage).

Heated discussion ensues—Moussa, who has been observ-ing, doesn't think it possible to fulfill Ralph's request. Others think

The theatrical curtain made of naked bedsprings. Photograph by T. Charles Erickson.

it possible if the steps are slightly altered. Ralph offers a new bit—a little fall forward with two tripping steps—to fill out a pause, but this creates more problems instead of solving them. Communication between the Africans and the Americans is awkward, not just because of the difference between French and English, but also because of the differences in the ways the two groups think about rhythm and music. In an ideal world we'd have hired an ethnomusicologist as well as an interpreter. Orida explains to me, "In Africa they don't count music the same way Western dancers do; they *sing* the rhythm instead." So what for Ralph seemed a simple mathematical exercise (A plus B must equal B plus A) was, for the Africans, a much more radical request to alter the whole syntax of a song.

Finally the four dancers finish together consistently, and jubilation reigns: after head-crunching work, a sweet reward. Ralph has each of them create several more steps in the same style, and with the mood they're all in, the choreography flows freely. By the time the week is out, the quartet has grown into an even more complex affair, with an "AB/BA, C, DE/ED" structure and a changing floor pattern.

THE WALKING IMPROVISATION

Ralph begins experimenting with a Walking Improvisation. He tells the dancers: just walk and stop, in the space, as yourself, observing the entire group. Nothing more. The men seem strangely isolated and sad while executing these instructions. Afterward we discuss how they felt and find that each dancer had his own particular conception of what was going on. James would walk until he hit up against an "invisible wall," then turn to find a new path. Angelo felt that he was walking alone, with spirits—the others were serving as spirits, and he imagined that only he could see them. Carlos, as the sole American participating, had the sensation that he was both on the inside and the outside at once: "I'm among my brothers, but I'm also alone."

Inspired by this image, Tracie, Peter and Ralph discuss the possibility that our Orestes figure could be created cumulatively, by everyone on stage. In this exercise everyone seems lost, everyone seems in exile from his true home. The African-Americans are not the only ones with a history of dislocation; years of colonialism have dislocated Africans as well. So can't everyone partake in an element of Orestes' character? Nothing is decided, but the idea is duly noted.

Saturday morning before rehearsal Ralph and I discuss potential problems. We spend time wondering whether Moussa is overly frustrated by the working process. He's in the minority as a Guinean dancer, and Ivoirean styles are clearly privileged in the choreography so far. It must be a humbling experience, as the eldest among them, to be asked to execute steps with which he's not very familiar and in which the others excel. Apparently there have also been problems with the drumming during Moussa's solo improvisations—Tapé and Goulei are either unwilling or unable to mark his steps properly, since he's dancing in a Guinean style. Moussa hadn't wanted to complain to Ralph, saying, "The Africans will work this out among themselves," but the whole story has been leaked to us by his wife, Orida. We've been so hyper-alert to possible cultural clashes between Americans and Africans that we completely missed the clash between Guineans and Ivoireans.

June 9–10

Rehearsals start up again with a dose of aggressive Monday morning energy, after our one precious day of rest. Ralph continues refining and extending the Collage and Quartet Phrases.

TRANCE DANCING

In the afternoon Ralph sits everyone down on the edge of the stage to broach the topic of Trance Dancing. He plays a video of *Divine Horsemen*, Maya Deren's black and white film of trance ceremonies in Haiti (shot in 1947–51 and edited posthumously). He indicates the dancers who rock, flail and stumble, eyes rolling to the back of their heads. These are the ones who have fallen into a trance. Ralph stops the tape and asks the men to divide up into pairs. "I want you to find out what this kind of energy means for each of you. Take turns—one partner will support the other so that he can move

freely, without falling. Don't imitate what you saw on the videotape—find an individual translation that makes sense to you."

The dancers first look reluctant, then outright refuse to
undertake the exercise. We stop everything and sit to discuss.
Djédjé explains that what Ralph is asking for is extremely complex: trance is very real, it's dangerous, and you don't just leap in
without any controls. Ralph replies that he's not interested in the
trance per se but in the physicality that comes out of it. When
Orida translates this last sentence, Nai and Angelo laugh out loud.
Ralph pushes on; he indicates the movement of one particular
trance dancer on the video monitor. This movement inspires him
because it suggests an incredible freedom, the freedom of letting
go. The motion is not even on the rhythm; it is loosed from all
constraints. But Djédjé points out that the film proceeds in slow
motion and the drums have been added in real time, on top of that.
"The rhythm you are hearing, Ralph, is not the rhythm to which
the dancer is dancing. If you watch the drummer in the background and look when the drumstick comes down, you'll see that
the dancer is actually with the beat."

Djédjé asks if Ralph wants them to dance in imitation of a
trance—much as in a play, when the character commits a murder
and the actor imitates the required action. Ralph says no and reit-
erates that it's the very *real* freedom of trance physicality that interests him. Tracie Morris intercedes, saying, "There is no freedom
in trance physicality. It's not a liberation from the body. Rather,
these folks are being mounted by a God. It isn't abandon, even
though it may look like it—rather, the body is being transformed
by an outside force. There's no liberty there." The dancers all agree
with Tracie.

Ralph tries a different tack. He clarifies: he's not interested
in putting either real trance or fake trance on stage. He's interested
in something that's related but different. He reaches for a new
example: "The last time I saw you all dance the Collage Phrase,

I experienced something related to total possession. The body lets go, gives itself over to something else. If we take these moments of freedom, and make them into a larger system . . ."

James interrupts. He's been standing apart, silent until now. "If I started moving and all of a sudden I was not able to control myself, no one here would be able to stop me. What you would need to get me out of it, you don't have in this country!" James's comment unleashes a flood of examples from the other dancers: once Nai went into a trance and took four hours to come out. Once a friend of Moussa's family went into a trance while alone, fell into some water, and drowned. And more. Ralph, tenacious to the end, finally realizes what a massive can of worms he's pried open. "I apologize!" he says in both French and English. "I was being naive . . . I obviously need to think about it some more. I've only looked at it from the outside, and you all have experienced it. Let me rethink my request, and get back to you."

The following afternoon we sit down and Ralph offers the following:

> I went home and thought about the issues. I think it's an area that you, as artists, cannot keep separate from real life. Maybe for you there is no other realm besides either being in a real trance or faking it. But Carlos and I have been discussing a certain kind of freedom we can access. Because we are Americans and don't have the same spiritual context, it's easier for us to access otherworldly movement without being either imitative or going into a trance. I saw the Haitian video-tape, and I admit, I wanted to exploit it, because it is visually engaging. I wanted to take from what I saw. So, now I would like to turn things around. I'd like you all to watch Carlos improvise with his house dancing, and tell me what *you* see.

Ralph instructs Carlos to improvise until he's "in a zone" and then see what happens. The instruction is tailored to Carlos, who does a large portion of his dancing in late-night clubs. He's told us before about the "zone" he needs to find in order to do his best work. But the results, in this setting, are inconclusive. Carlos stops the improvisation, saying he feels completely lost. James jumps on the comment: "Yes, exactly—he was lost because he started to go—that's what falling into a trance is!"

I ask Ralph if he'd consider doing this exercise as well, so the Africans can see what he means directly, from his body. He hesitates, then agrees. He also decides that he and Carlos will put on the rehearsal suits before they try again. As he dons his rehearsal suit, he catches my eye and says, only half-joking, "You'll pay for this later, Katherine!" Ralph the director, who has spent weeks controlling and shaping this rehearsal process, will now stand in front of his dancers and try to demonstrate a loss of control.

The results are again inconclusive. Sometimes Carlos or Ralph demonstrates a burst of incredible energy, at other times they proceed in their usual improvisational mode. Ralph dances in his signature style, though he is a little larger, a little more dangerous than usual. Carlos seems troubled and bows out early; Ralph continues, then holds still for a long moment, then continues briefly before stopping. In the discussion afterward, Djédjé asks Carlos and Ralph why they stopped when they did. Carlos explains that he was disoriented. Ralph says he stopped because he was tired but that he would be interested in continuing beyond that point at another time. Djédjé tells him that's exactly where the trance energy is: on the other side of the fatigue. In general, the Africans are responding to this experiment as if Ralph and Carlos had been playing on the edges of real trance. Ralph has not managed to convey his concept of another category of movement, one in which there is freedom but no danger.

Djédjé offers some analysis, saying that Ralph was in more

*Goulei Tchépoho (against the wall) and Akpa Yves Didier ("James"). Photograph by
T. Charles Erickson.*

control than Carlos because he had a mental image of what he
wanted from the exercise. Whenever things got out of control, he
could return to his image, whereas Carlos had no image to anchor
him. Thus Carlos was in more danger of falling into a trance than
Ralph. Moussa agrees, adding that while Ralph was letting his
muscles go free, internally he always knew where he was going.
Ralph latches on to this distinction and asks them to keep thinking about the problem in those terms: muscles in a free physical
form, rather than the mind or spirit in trance. Moussa replies that
it could be done, but it would be difficult for them, as it would
require them to make a separation between the spiritual and the
physical. At this point Jenny Friend (our stage manager) inter-

rupts—we've gone overtime with this discussion, the rehearsal is officially long over. Ralph asks the dancers to consider whether this kind of work could be done and to tell him what they would require to be comfortable undertaking it.

After the dancers have left, Ralph, Peter and I sit in the empty space and talk about what just happened. Is Ralph's request simply too dangerous? Is it inherently improper? Does it encroach upon the third circle of African dance that Djédjé mentioned on the first day? Ralph decides that although he has been clumsy, he shouldn't shy off and abandon his train of thought completely. Moussa's comment has given him a way to approach his idea physically, not spiritually. He'll proceed with care, trusting the dancers to define what is and is not appropriate.

June 10–11

Stan Pressner, our lighting designer, visits the workshop. During a lunch break we stay to look at lighting ideas. Over the last week Nari Ward has hung up a few sets of naked bedsprings with bits of fabric woven sparsely into the wire. He plans to create a complete theatrical curtain out of these bedsprings. Stan carries a single light around the space, aiming it at the makeshift curtain from different angles. The springs can be translucent or transparent, depending on how they're lit. Nari, Stan and Ralph discuss how to create a prologue feel for the opening of the piece. Nari and Ralph want to start with several layers of bedspring curtains and gradually reveal the space as the curtains fly out one by one.

One of the first premises about this set is that it won't really *be* a set but rather a sculptural installation for a theatrical space. Nari and Ralph describe how the entire stage will be open and "raw"— we'll see the bricks of the back wall, the stairs to the flies, the door to the shop. All will be revealed; theatrical artifice will be avoided.

Stan appreciates the idea but warns Ralph that there will be no tidy places to hide the lights. All the instruments will be present. Even more importantly, every wall that the light hits will be present. Ralph and Stan briefly discuss different possibilities for using masking, but Ralph decides to stick with the challenge of a completely open space.

We look at Nari's second major set element: a curtain composed entirely of empty bottles, held together by thin cables, which will rise from piles on the ground during the final section of the piece. Again the production crew has realized just a small section of what will ultimately become, if all approve, a full-size stage curtain. Stan carries around his single light again, trying out different angles. It's soon obvious that light shining on glass will be beautiful from almost any angle.

June 12

During warm-up there is lively discussion of the fifth game of the NBA finals last night. We've been following every game, and the entire cast and crew, with the exception of poor Wier Harman (the assistant director for the workshop period and a loyal Jazz fan), root for the Bulls. This morning no one can stop talking about Michael Jordan. He was stricken with the flu, looked dog-tired on the bench, but once on the court he somehow summoned the energy to make over thirty points and lead his team to victory. We all agree that Michael Jordan is a superhuman being and decide that today's rehearsal will be dedicated to him. Ralph jokes about doing our yoga breathing while chanting: "Jordan Jordan Jordan," once on each exhale.

Today begins with a free improvisation session, returning to the pattern of the first week's work. The dancers are given no specific instructions except to make sure to watch each other. It takes a few turns before things get going, but soon each dancer is warming up the room a notch more than the previous dancer. The mood is aggressive, competitive and terribly playful. Orida runs up on stage to put a dollar bill on Goulei's forehead, where it sticks because of the sweat. Is today's improv so amazing because Ralph asked them to return to what they know best, after a week of difficult, unfamiliar work? Or perhaps it's due to the lingering image of Michael Jordan pulling a superhuman performance out of thin air? As I write "THIS IS HOT" in big letters in my notebook, Ralph comes up beside me and exclaims, "Postmodern dance is so *boring*. This reminds me what dance is all about!"

In the early afternoon Francisco López arrives. He's an experimental composer from Spain, one of two composers who will collaborate on *Geography* (the other is the New Yorker Paul D. Miller, aka DJ Spooky, who is still away on tour). Reading his bio, I'm intrigued to discover that Francisco has a second career as a professor of entomology (the study of insects). In fact, he's stopping off to join us in New Haven on his way to do research in the Central American rain forests.

Francisco observes silently throughout the day, then after the dinner break Ralph presents him to the company and asks him to introduce his work. Francisco begins by holding up one of the drums and making an analogy: just as this instrument is made of natural materials (wood, goatskin), and with it one can play whatever one likes, so his music is made by recording sounds from nature and arranging them as he likes. His music isn't made to dance to, since it has no particular rhythm, but one *can* dance to it. After that preface Francisco asks that we turn off the lights and listen in the dark. He plays several tracks, mixing them carefully on the sound board in front of him. We hear incredibly dense, layered soundscapes; some are haunting and wistful, while others have a menacing, industrial quality. All make use of a full range of volume, and at points become extremely loud, almost overwhelming.

Afterward the lights come back on and Ralph asks for reactions. Nai begins:

> It made us travel: to a big factory where a lot of people are working, or to the middle of the bush, in Nature.

The dancers all chime in: they heard a plane passing far away, insects in the bush, a sawmill, a drum in the distance, rain, wind. Djédjé offers his analysis:

> I noticed that you've made something that reflects what Ralph is doing. You transport us to an African world which is a developed world—you can take us from deep in the bush immediately into a world with machines. I relate this to what Ralph is trying to do by using African forms and modern dance forms to make something entirely new.

Everyone excitedly agrees. Francisco's music doesn't create an easy opposition between nature and technology—instead, it slides them together until one can hear both in a single passage. In his work so far Ralph has been nurturing a similar relationship between African and American styles of dance.

June 13

Midway into the afternoon's rehearsal Ralph dismisses all the cast except Moussa, James and Carlos in order to continue work on the idea of Trance Dancing. Really by now we need another way to describe this idea of Ralph's, since "trance" has proven inappropriate, but as no one has come up with a good substitute, we surround the term with implicit quotation marks.

After reiterating that he's interested in a freer physical form and not an actual trance, Ralph gives the three dancers their instructions. They are to begin walking in simple paths, upstage and downstage. Their movement will gradually grow larger, but they may take as long as they like to let it grow—they could take two days if need be. The important thing is that they not imitate a preconceived idea, that their movement be as free as possible. They may keep their eyes closed if they like. Ralph asks if there are any objections to undertaking the exercise in this way; there are none. Francisco puts on a piece of his music and we dim the lights. Ralph joins the three on the stage. Four dancers, blind to the world, stumble freely forward and back.

From the very first, James's path is not straight. He often wanders into Ralph's neighboring area. As the movement starts to grow larger, James stumbles completely outside of the established structure, into other areas of the stage. He comes into contact with other dancers and changes them. Now all four are cut loose from their paths, exploring the entire space. Their eyes remain closed, and all the observers hurriedly congregate at the downstage lip of the stage, ready to catch anyone who wanders too far astray.

Ralph's idea of neutral (or his "resting position") is a recognizable form. Whenever he stops moving, he sits very still and straight, composing himself, making a "blank slate" before starting to move again. Moussa and James's ideas of neutral aren't found in one particular form. Their neutrals are anywhere or nowhere. If their energy dies down, they rest in whatever position they happen to find themselves. They are much more interesting to watch than Ralph or Carlos, but also more frightening. James, especially, is scaring me. I remember his warning: "If I started moving and all of a sudden I was not able to control myself, no one here would be able to stop me!" After about a half-hour, Ralph pulls himself out of the exercise. Orida goes up to each of the remaining three dancers and whispers softly in his ear. They stop, sit down, and slowly reenter the mundane world. No one speaks for several minutes.

Ralph asks James if he's all right. James replies that he's nauseous and his head hurts, but beyond that, he feels okay about doing this kind of work. He can keep himself safe, especially if he makes some extra sacrifices to protect himself, which he'll do when he goes back to the Côte d'Ivoire after the workshop. Carlos and Moussa also feel nauseous, and Ralph decides that they shouldn't keep their eyes closed in the future—that's the source of the nausea. We end work for the day without further discussion.

June 14

The Literary Managers and Dramaturgs of the Americas (LMDA) conference is hosted at Yale today, and we hold an open rehearsal for conference attendees. As morning warm-up finishes, the LMDA folks start filtering into the house. I'm still onstage doing handstands with the dancers, as I do at the close of every warm-up. Catherine Sheehy sidles up to me and teases, "That's the way to demonstrate the role of the dramaturg!"

THE MINUET

Ralph decides to show our guests a rehearsal of the Minuet section. This is an idea he's been putting together gradually over the last two weeks. It began with stage-combat falls between Angelo and Djédjé—one dancer takes the other by the lapels of his suit jacket, hurling him into the air and down flat on his back. Ralph then set that explosive bit of violence within a very stately duet based on the traditional minuet. As a harpsichord plunks out the proper tones of a Bach prelude, the two men meet at center stage,

①

STRAW - with cheese cloth veil

over view

② FELT

③

FELT - with light, thread / fringe

over view

④

Linen? - ½" seams standing upon outside of cap.

BACK with elastic covered with fabric

Liz Prince's sketches of proposed costume pieces.

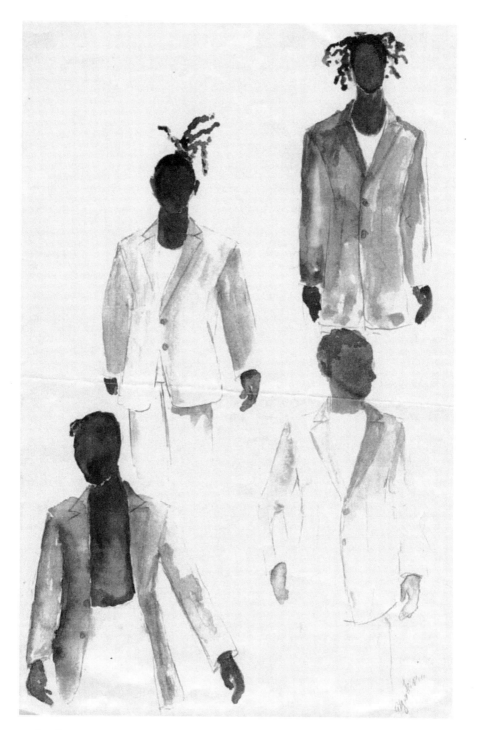

Liz Prince's costume sketches.

execute a few carefully elegant steps and then burst into violent action. When the fall is complete, the downed partner recovers, the other partner gently helping him up. Then they recommence the minuet, this time reversing the roles so that the previous aggressor is the present victim.

Ralph, Angelo and Djédjé have developed an image that refers, quite succinctly, to the dynamics of violence in a postcolonial state. The colonizer is long gone, but his presence lingers on through his aesthetic standards and his sense of decorum, as symbolized by the minuet. The two brothers, countrymen, alternate between collaborating on the dance, attacking each other, and helping each other up. Each phase of their relationship has equal weight, and the Bach music continues indifferently, no matter what happens to them. Yet this music, however oppressive its role in context, also lends a mournful beauty to the entire chain of events. The image is simple, but the resonances are complex. We've all fallen in love with this bit of choreography.

Now Ralph shows a longer version of the Minuet, in which two more dancers enter, forming two simultaneous duets, later followed by two more dancers, and the group creates two simultaneous trios. In this last part three dancers huddle together in a standing wrestling clinch—still but tense, full of potential energy. On a predetermined signal the clinch explodes into a rolling, tumbling mess. Each dancer falls in his own direction. When all are still, the dancers get up, slowly and do it all over again. After running the whole series once, Ralph instructs the dancers not to "play dead" after the falls. "Get up slowly, but right away—always be moving. The point is not to layer any extra drama over the top of this. The energy *is* the drama."

June 17

The day starts early with a large production meeting, crowded around the conference table in the technical design room. DJ Spooky has just arrived from New York; this meeting is his first taste of the *Geography* project, apart from his conversations with Ralph.

Ben Sammler (Yale Rep production supervisor), Ralph and the designers start by pinning down the time when certain decisions will have to be made in order for budgeting and construction to proceed on the usual Yale Rep schedule. Ralph, in love with the gradually unfolding rehearsal process, wants to hold off on final decisions as long as he possibly can. But the assumptions of the dance world, where development of a piece can take over a year, don't quite match the assumptions of the resident theatre world, where rehearsal periods average four to six weeks, and most production decisions are made before the actors even arrive. Yet I sense no unpleasant tension—Yale is as accommodating as it can be to Ralph's process, and Ralph recognizes his limits.

We turn to the scale set model that's been built by Adam Stockhausen, a Yale student designer. On the stage floor sit miniature A-frame ladders wrapped in fabric, and piles of miniature glass bottles lie ready to fly up and form a curtain later on. An oversized ceiling fan made from fragmented ladders hovers over the center of the stage. Three curtains of miniature bedsprings can be inserted and removed. Nari explains that he hopes to wrap or otherwise alter all onstage objects—for instance, the African drums and the microphone stands—so that nothing on stage will make a direct reference to the outside world. After the meeting officially concludes, the entire design team and technical staff remain huddled around the set model like kids around a dollhouse, making small adjustments and discussing options.

As we've planned an informal showing for the collaborators today, the first portion of rehearsal is spent setting a show order.

Collage and Quartet have been greatly extended so that the four dancers of the Quartet become two (James and Angelo) and then the two become one (Angelo). At the close of this progression Angelo will perform a short solo to the African drums, followed by Ralph, who will do the same. Then the stage will clear and the drummers will play a four minute Drum Quartet, composed by Moussa and featuring a drum solo by Tapé.

ROCK THROWING

Another section begins with the "Overview" text, which segues into the Minuet, which then segues into our new Rock Throwing episode. Experimenting with the two drummers and using palm-sized rocks and a plywood wall, Ralph lands on the image of Tapé standing at the wall, two rocks in hand, moving back and forth and drumming on the plywood, while Goulei (carefully!) throws more rocks at the wall around him. The rocks hit hard, but Goulei's aim is sharp, and Tapé remains unscathed. (All the same, this section makes Jenny Friend extremely nervous.)

Today, however, Tapé is laid up at home with a pulled muscle. Ralph decides that he will take Tapé's place against the wall for the showing, but he needs to practice first. He flinches as Goulei hurls the first rocks in his direction, and the rest of the cast laughs. Soon he gets the hang of it. During a break just afterward Ralph and I discuss the possibility of his taking over Tapé's role permanently. I suggest that if *Geography* is in some measure his story, then it makes sense for him to put himself in the hot seat. Ralph agrees. It is unclear whether the rock-throwing indicates a punishment for an earlier crime or a crime in itself, but that ambiguity, it turns out, is exactly what Ralph likes. Is it a stoning? Is it two boys playing games? Is it two percussionists playing with the sound of rocks against wood? Ralph wants all these readings to be equally present.

SINGING ON LADDERS AND
MOUSSA'S SOLO

We will also present a few musical selections. Djédjé has been
rehearsing a contemporary African song for solo voice and chorus,
which the dancers sing while perched atop Nari's wrapped A-
frame ladders. Today we'll try an impromptu experiment whereby
Djédjé's song will be overlapped by a song that Tracie has written
for Moussa, in an African-American blues idiom.

Moussa also has a new solo near the top of the show, right
after Ralph's "Intro/Outro" poem (now called Map). During
today's showing I see it for the first time. He enters in silence,
alone, a Guinean *dundun* drum slung across his shoulders. First he
plays a powerful solo, then carefully places drum and drumsticks
on the floor, walks a few steps away, and bursts into a full-energy
dance. He's in his element during the dance, using all the steps that
he knows and loves. Then, very simply, he repeats: one more un-
danced drum solo, one more silent dance solo. At the end he picks
up the drum and walks off. By separating and alternating African
dance and African drumming—two elements that usually go
together—Moussa's Solo sends a strong signal to the audience. It
warns that we're in a world where traditional forms can be taken
apart and experimented with. And on a more emotional level, it
conveys a slight unease, the sense that a familiar association is now
dislocated. We imagine the elements together, but watch them
separately. As if Moussa is attempting an impossible task—to dance
to his own drumming—and failing gloriously.

After the showing is complete the dancers file out for dinner break and Ralph meets with the collaborators. One topic of
discussion is narrative, or the current lack thereof. Ralph explains
that the focus of the primary workshop has been to find out how
this particular group of men can work together. He plans to spend
time after this workshop and before the next formulating the more

Liz Prince's sketches of the gowns.

comprehensive narrative structure, and the work from August on should move in that direction. Peter points out that in what we've just seen, the text doesn't seem very integrated into the rest of the piece. Perhaps when a narrative structure has been decided upon, Tracie's text will fall into place as part of a larger scheme.

We haven't shown any of the experiments with Trance Dancing (or as we're now starting to call it, Meditation Dancing), but Ralph is eager to describe this work to the designers. He wants to pursue the idea as part of the final Divination section, after the bottle curtains have risen into the air; he's looking for material powerful enough to share space with the bottles. But if the Meditation Dance were staged, could we keep the dancers safe? One suggestion is to have stagehands stand at the front lip of the stage, just as the observers did spontaneously in rehearsal. Ralph and Nari also briefly consider creating a netted-in area at the back of the stage—an enclosure within which it would be impossible to hurt one's self.

Tracie brings up the singing experiment, which, she freely admits, didn't work at all. Djédjé drowned out Moussa's song, and the two melodies didn't overlap in an interesting fashion. They just turned into noise. However, with time, they could work out the balance and find ways for the two melodies to interrelate. She's eager to continue work on this idea.

The dancers come back from dinner and we ask for their feedback. Angelo is inspired by the fact that the show is starting to take shape. He quotes a proverb: *C'est en mangeant que l'appetit vient* (Eating brings on the appetite), and tells Ralph that the more specific their instructions, the further they can go. Djédjé is similarly enthusiastic, but he's also concerned that the dancers don't fully understand the manner in which they should perform this material:

DJÉDJÉ: We, in other words the dancers from Africa, are used to
dancing with spirits. You saw this, Ralph, and liked it about

us. . . . Here we are trying to do an amalgam of steps from us and you both. I don't know, should I use my own system of dancing to dance them, or another more disassociated way? I think the confusion keeps us from giving all of our energy, because we feel cut off from part of ourselves.

RALPH: We need to look at this question. I want you to show me physically what you mean. Everyone should be dancing as themselves, no matter what. But it's a question of what kind of performance is appropriate at a given time. And I want you and everyone else to always feel connected, physically and emotionally, to what you're doing on stage.

June 18

THE CIRCLE DANCES

Today Ralph wants to explore something completely new. He asks the Africans if they know any traditional dances for a group of people together in a circle. The answer is, "Of course." Over the next few hours we look at many different circle dances and take time to hear about the cultural contexts for each. The dancers enjoy explaining their heritage to the uninformed Americans—especially James, who relates the contexts for several dances in exquisite detail. Then Ralph picks a dance from each dancer and asks him to teach a few steps to the rest of the group. From Moussa he chooses the Makuru, a festival dance from the Susu people, danced to celebrate the rice harvest. From James he chooses the Namboro, which means "strong men"—in it the male dancers keep their arms raised and flexed, trembling with strength. Angelo offers part of the Goli, a nonsacred mask dance from the Baule people. And from Nai and Djédjé we get the Zoah, a general celebration dance used by women in the Côte d'Ivoire. The dancers sing to accompany the dances—either formal songs with lyrics or vocal imitations of the appropriate instruments. The drummers do not play for this exercise; all sound is generated by the dancers themselves.

After they've mastered each other's steps, Ralph asks them to meet in a circle for the first dance, stop on a cue, walk apart and around the space and reconvene in the center to begin the next dance. This pattern repeats. As they walk apart, the dancers follow the same instructions they followed during the Walking Improvisation, several weeks ago. The effect is an intermittent sense of community—the group coheres, celebrates, and then dissipates into everyday solitude. And although the Circle Dances are joyous, they do not open out to the audience and include the observer in the communal feeling. In his shaping of this material Ralph has managed to evoke a sense of dislocation similar to what I felt watching Moussa's Solo yesterday. Yet there is no denying that the dancers' mood, when they find themselves back in the circle again, is celebratory.

June 19

MOUSSA'S BLUES SONG

Tracie has the run of this evening's rehearsal in order to work on her blues song for Moussa and chorus. For now all the dancers will learn it in English. Orida and I pass out copies of our French translation, and Orida glosses the English lyrics. She explains that the protagonist of Tracie's song is someone who feels uprooted, cut off from his origins.

Tracie plays a tape of her own voice singing the song and asks them to imitate her strong, clear tones. Moussa's voice will lead, and the chorus will reply in unison. We try this through several times, and the results are awkward, tentative. Tracie promises that, as Angelo has already requested, a choral director will come to work with them. For now she asks Peter to drill the pronunciation of the more problematic English words.

I walk away from the stage and into the house, and when I turn around to get a glimpse of the picture behind me, I am shocked: there, framed perfectly in the proscenium, is the image of a colonial schoolroom, with Peter slowly articulating English words and a class full of African men repeating after him in unison. I know this image is not either Tracie's or Peter's intent, but I can't quite shake the impression it leaves. Why are we asking these artists to perform in a language that feels so foreign to them?

After hours Peter, Tracie, Ralph and I sit down to discuss Moussa's song. Peter and I both feel strongly that we shouldn't be asking the performers to do so much work in a language they don't know. Ralph agrees and adds that Moussa singing in English sounds like a parody of a pop song, probably because that's the English idiom he knows best. Why aren't we asking him to sing in French or Susu, with which he has a more organic connection? Tracie replies that she has no problem creating a song in French or Susu, but she was trying to create something accessible to an English-speaking audience. Moussa speaks a little English already, so it's not as much of a stretch for him. Tracie listens to all our weighty concerns but is not inclined to give up easily. She asks us to reserve final judgment until after the choral director comes.

June 21

Ralph is eager to broach all new ideas in the precious few days that remain of the workshop. Even if there's not enough time to see an idea through, he will at least have a concrete image to ponder over the next two months, before workshops start up again.

RITUAL   WITH   THE   ROCKS

Today we experiment with DJ Spooky's contribution: two sets of
motion detectors mounted on aluminum walkers. The dancers will
trigger an alarm whenever they cross the invisible beam determined by each set of equipment. However, DJ Spooky and sound
designer Rob Gorton have substituted a number of different audio
samples for the usual shrill alarm. Now when a dancer crosses the
sensor beam, we hear a bird call or a burst of the drums or the
sound of the rocks being thrown against the plywood wall.
Occasionally the sample is of the original alarm, too.

Ralph tells the dancers to create their own private rituals in
the space. As working material, he asks them to use the rocks, just
picking up one or two at a time. And he urges them to think of
the stage, rocks and set pieces as their entire world. Liz Prince sends
two muslin dress mock-ups from New York, and Ralph asks the
dancers to try them on for this exercise.

After hours of work in this vein Ralph discovers a promising image: James and Angelo, wearing the gowns, execute a home-
made ritual wherein they throw a rock, slowly walk toward it, pick
it up and start again. These two dancers, more than the others, are
able to hold our focus while they do next to nothing. Their energy
is clear, strong, deliberate, simple. In the long white muslin dresses
they seem ethereal, like walking spirits. And every time they cross
one of the sensor beams, they trigger a gentle bird call or a blaring
alarm. I'm not sure what it means, but it is strangely compelling.
Moussa says he is reminded of ghosts haunting graveyards.

After dinner break the company members report to the base-
ment space to work with a choral director. She stands behind a
sophisticated electronic keyboard and starts by giving them point-
ers on how to warm up their voices. An excruciating sort of
progress is made. She helps Moussa, Angelo and James establish a
clear melody for Moussa's song. But when she asks Djédjé, Nai and

Liz Prince's costume sketch.

Tapé to sing the contemporary African song at the same time, it just doesn't work. They try it several times, and the overlap is never interesting, it's always just noise. It won't ever work. Ralph asks Tapé, "What did you think . . . honestly?" and Tapé declines to say. We all laugh because the answer is clear, though Tapé refuses to say it aloud. He just rubs his chin and says, "Hmmmm. . . ." Everyone in the room can fill in the blanks.

June 23: Last day of the workshop

By happy coincidence, the Ki-Yi M'Bock company is in New Haven this week, performing at the International Festival of Arts and Ideas. The entire company, including WereWere Liking, who serves as both spiritual leader and artistic director, will be able to observe our final "open rehearsal." As the *Geography* company begins its last yoga warm-up until August, WereWere and her assistant are already installed in the audience. WereWere is a large, regal woman in traditional African dress. A beautifully carved mahogany staff rests against the seat next to her and a Powerbook computer is open on her lap. She's finishing up some paperwork for her own show while watching Djédjé, Nai, Tapé and Goulei out of the corner of her eye.

Soon WereWere is joined by the members of her company, members of the Yale Drama School community, interested parties up from New York and friends the dancers have made during their four weeks here. We present almost the same material from the showing a week ago, with the addition of the Circle Dances and James and Angelo's Ritual with the Rocks.

After the showing WereWere and Ralph meet for a lengthy conversation. She is supportive and congratulatory, telling Ralph that he's gotten exceptional work out of Djédjé and Nai. I overhear her describing her reaction to Ralph's own dancing: "I had an image of you in the middle of your solo—I saw you as a little flame passing through a tunnel." Ralph is standing quite close to WereWere. I wander away, leaving the two of them alone.

The company returns later for closing words. Each cast member speaks long and eloquently on what the experience has meant so far. Ralph shares feedback he received from another member of Ki-Yi, who told him the work was "mystical and dangerous." He considers that a great compliment. He congratulates and thanks the dancers for taking so many risks with him. Nai tells the company, "We're going to leave a mark on people." James chimes in, slightly contrary, saying that he has a good conception of the piece but he doesn't yet have what he wants. Ralph laughs and says, "Me too."

July 1997

Ralph and I meet at a café in New York. I bring the final copy of my rehearsal logbook—169 typed pages of observations on both the work in progress and our rehearsal-room chemistry—and set it down on his side of the table with a large thunk. He'll read through it over the next month. Our assumption is that the dynamics of collaboration have become part of the subject matter of *Geography,* and our hope is that the logbook will help Ralph make this fact even more explicit.

We discuss my evolving role in the rehearsal room. During the next group of workshops and rehearsals I will phase out of my role as anthropologist/observer and try to be less absorbed in the details, so that I may provide useful feedback on the larger picture—on *Geography* as a work of art rather than a working process. I had also been spending an increasing portion of my day as second-string interpreter, and while I rather enjoy the role, we discuss how to limit this involvement.

I'm eager to hear Ralph's thoughts on *The Oresteia* narrative and how he plans to work it more explicitly into the material we've generated so far. It soon becomes clear that actually narrating *The Oresteia* is less and less of a priority for Ralph—if it ever was one. I realize that we're never going to tell the tale in the way I'd first imagined and that I must adjust my assumptions to match the real course of Ralph's inspiration. He's not interested in making these dancers into distinct characters (although at one point early on there had been a cast list: Moussa as Agamemnon, Djédjé as Aegisthus, and so on). He's not interested in a chain of interactions with clear befores and afters. He continues to work with the image of Orestes in exile, with the idea of Orestes' crime (though for Ralph the exact nature of the crime remains mysterious) and with a progression toward a trial followed by a (temporary?) release from the cycle of violence. But these narrative elements feed him poetically; they are not the literal substance of what he wants to convey to the audience. They live below, rather than on, the surface.

Ralph is happy with the skeleton of a piece created so far. Back in June he divided Orestes' saga into four parts in order to give the work an overall structure. The first three parts—Map, Crime and Trial—are pretty well sketched out. The main work before him is to choreograph the final section, Divination. The lack of time is frustrating: with so much work left to do to understand the beginning, how can he know what kind of end is required? Originally the Meditation Dancing was to be the major element in this final section, but now he's wondering if it can ever be staged—it's too diffuse and too unpredictable. If he can't figure out a way to make it work, he'll need a new idea.

August 24–September 20

The African performers return to the United States after a month back home in Abidjan. The company assembles for two weeks of workshop at Art Awareness, a bucolic arts complex in the Catskill Mountains. This is followed by two weeks of workshop at the Brooklyn Academy of Music, courtesy of the 651 organization. I join for the first week of the first workshop and visit the Brooklyn workshop intermittently.

At Art Awareness we spend much time and energy to recreate what was achieved at the end of the first workshop. Everyone's memory is slightly different, and it's frustrating how much has been lost. We double back, using the videos to clarify and reteach every last detail of the choreography.

TIRE TALK

Tracie and Ralph have developed new ideas, one being to stage a group conversation with all members of the company sitting in a circle on stools Nari has built from old piled-up tires. For this idea Tracie has written a sound poem using the small interjections she's overheard in the company's everyday speech. She imagines the group operating like a Greek chorus, commenting upon the action. Though the subject of their discussion will remain abstract to the audience, at the end of the segment it will be clear that they've reached an agreement. We rehearse this over an afternoon, first assigning words and then trying to orchestrate the rhythms of a real conversation.

When I see this section again in Brooklyn, the poem has disappeared. Ralph found it too carefully composed and was more interested in the unruly rhythms of the cast's actual speech. Now the cast will enter into a real argument on stage. Tracie provides them with a subject—capital punishment—and assigns who is pro, con and undecided. Ralph asks the company to discuss it freely in whatever language they choose—French, English or their native tongues. There are a few set cues: Angelo begins the discussion explosively, internal cues modulate the volume and then a subtle cue from Nai tells them to stop and sit in heavy silence before getting up and rolling the tire stools away. Otherwise the argument is theirs to conduct as they wish. Ralph is also part of the gathering but says very little. He places this new Tire Talk episode at the head of the Trial section, after the "Overview" poem. The implication is that the entire company is deciding Ralph/Orestes' fate.

CIRCLE DANCES WITH SATELLITES

Also in Brooklyn, Ralph continues work on the Circle Dance section. While the Africans dance traditional steps in their own celebratory but self-contained circle, Carlos and Ralph dance in the
contemporary American vein, one on either side of the central
area, pushed off to the edges of the stage. Carlos and Ralph are in
unison but separated from each other, and their choreography
includes trips and falls and off-balance movements. When the
Africans break apart into the walking section, they make eye contact with Ralph and Carlos, but they always reconstitute in the
center while Ralph and Carlos remain on the margins. The
Africans form a central group but remain closed to the (American)
audience; the Americans are open to the audience but separated,
alone. Ralph calls himself and Carlos the Satellites to the Africans'
Circle Dances. The image evokes all the limits Ralph has found to
the ideals of cross-cultural collaboration and communication. I'm
reminded of a statement Ralph made before rehearsals had even
begun; he talked of the "separateness that exists between completely different black worlds."

It's getting easier and easier for Ralph to articulate his inspirational imagery. He clarifies: the crime at stake in this piece is,
above all else, the crime of putting his dancing and the Africans'
dancing together on the same stage. Many have told him that it
couldn't be done, that it would be impossible for him to choreograph for African dancers without being disrespectful of their culture. He tells the cast, "People said we could not dance together,
but we have anyway, and that is our crime."

Ralph also restates his understanding of the costumes. The
gowns represent his romanticized images of an African past: ances-
tors, spirits, race memory. The suits have a reciprocal relationship,
as they represent the Africans' romance of the American mystique:

power, money, big business.

Much progress is made in Brooklyn as the skeleton of a show begins to take on flesh. Unfortunately it's also the first time we experience serious discord. Minor disagreements regarding housing arrangements and transportation lead to the contracts being brought out for examination. Some of the dancers see these documents for the first time, since the two artistic directors in Abidjan had required that the contracts be drawn not with the individual dancers but with the dance companies. The original disputes are quickly settled, but the contracts also indicate that just half of each dancer's salary is being paid to him directly while the other half is being paid to his dance company in Abidjan. Angelo and James react to this information with outrage. Djédjé and the other members of Ki-Yi M'Bock were aware of this arrangement, but apparently Angelo and James were not. Their anger and disappointment are primarily aimed at Souleymane Koly, the director of the Ensemble Koteba, but also at the staff of Yale Rep and at MAPP. After these incidents a hint of distrust lingers between dancers and support staff—the overt issues are resolved, but a measure of innocence has been lost. The boundless good will of the first workshop has acquired boundaries.

September 15: The Judson Church showing

Near the end of the Brooklyn workshop Ralph presents a "work-in-progress showing" to the New York public under the auspices of Movement Research at the Judson Church. As the dancers warm up that evening, I explain that the Judson Church is a key location in the history of American dance. Here is the cauldron for the experimentation that thrived in the New York of the late 1960s and early 1970s. Here is where the early postmodern dancers showed their work: Yvonne Rainer, Steve Paxton, Trisha Brown,

The company. Photograph by T. Charles Erickson.

Meredith Monk. The names mean nothing to the Africans, but they appreciate the idea that their performance space could be haunted by some of Ralph's artistic forebears.

The program consists loosely of the first two sections of the final show: Map and Crime. The audience sits very close to the dancers; the drums are loud and the dancers' exertion is palpable. Finally the lights fade down slowly on Tapé alone, sitting by his *djembe*, whistling bird calls with uncanny verisimilitude. The man sitting behind me gasps audibly. A few seconds later, the entire audience is standing, cheering, yelping, clapping until their hands are sore. One friend of mine in the audience is crying. Another friend, a young African-American choreographer just starting his career in New York, tells me he's never seen a more intelligent piece about race. He identified with the material profoundly; he swears it encapsulated everything about how he sees himself and how others see him. As he speaks his hand hovers directly above his heart, and I am reminded that on however many different levels I may love and respond to this piece, there is another level I will never access directly, a level that touches deep-seated questions about African-American (especially African-American *male*) perceptions of self.

September 22-29: New Haven rehearsals begin

DIVINATION DANCE

Back at Yale our days take on a lot more urgency and a little less levity. The pressure is on. Ralph plunges into the new Divination choreography, which he had only just begun on the final days of the Brooklyn workshop.

To fashion this Divination Dance, Ralph combines the techniques he used successfully on the Path Phrase and the Collage Phrase. He improvises in front of the dancers and then videotapes them improvising their own variations on what he's just done. From the videotapes he selects sections of each dancer's movement and collages all the bits together. The result is the most thorough marriage of the two styles we've yet seen. The general energy of the movement is closer to Ralph's, but the shapes and rhythmical accents are perfectly suited to bodies trained in African dance. Ralph, watching a rehearsal, comments to me:

> I can't ask them for straight lines and pointed feet; nor would I want to. But by asking them to imitate me, I've found a way to ask them for broader, more elongated forms than they would have created on their own. It's interesting work, to draw that distinction— between an inappropriate request and an interesting translation.

It's also the kind of work that could only have happened this far into the rehearsal process. At this point the Africans and the Americans have seen so much of each other that their styles have become familiar unknowns.

TRIO FOR ANGELO, MOUSSA AND RALPH

Late one Saturday night Ralph tries an improvisational trio with Moussa, Angelo and himself, all wearing the white gowns. Moussa dances in several Guinean styles; Angelo in a single Baule style; and Ralph in his contemporary American style. The only accompaniment is Angelo's voice as he sings out the proper rhythm for his step. The three dancers remain in close proximity, with Ralph weaving through and around the other two. Come Monday morning Angelo has a new assignment: he must watch the video and learn to reproduce the structure of the improvisation—to know how long he spent on each step before going to the next. Moussa and Ralph will continue to improvise freely, but Angelo will become the regular "clock" to which they set their movement. Periodically Angelo will call out *"Moussa, on change"* (Moussa, change) to signify that Moussa should switch to a new step. Thus the entire episode is scored by Angelo, but within that form the performers will create anew each night. This section marks another achievement in our exploration of collaborative possibilities—it's the first time that Ralph's found a way for different styles, unaltered, to share the same space. The close conjunction of three very different dancing bodies fascinates me every time I watch it.

THE PROLOGUE

The drummers are the star players in Ralph's new prologue. The bedspring curtains are down as Tapé wanders out in a long "ancestor" gown, finds a place on the floor to sit, and begins playing with a single rock. First he hits it on the ground, once, twice; then he begins pounding out increasingly complicated rhythms. Goulei, also wearing his gown, enters. Tapé stops and stands. Goulei begins speaking to Tapé in hushed tones, so that only Tapé can hear him, walking closer and closer until he's speaking directly in Tapé's ear. He seems to be explaining or reprimanding. When he's done, Tapé hands Goulei the rock, like a guilty child handing over a forbidden object, and they both exit. This barest sketch of a scene introduces the *Geography* rock in all its ambivalent glory—is it an instrument of play or of violence? Ralph also likes the scene because it's "mysterious," and because it introduces the white-gowned ancestor figures, who won't truly emerge until the end of the Trial section. By putting them up front, they will seem to preside over the entire evening.

PURIFICATION

We look again at James and Angelo's Ritual with the Rocks, now positioned after the Rock Throwing scene with Ralph and Goulei. In the aftermath of the violent play, these two white-gowned figures emerge from the wings and pick up the rocks that now lie scattered. They pick them up one by one, reverently, and lob them one by one, watching to see where they land. They throw rocks in a completely different way than Goulei has thrown rocks just a moment before. Because of its relation to the previous episode, we're now calling their ritual Purification. But James and Angelo have some questions about how they are to perform this. Angelo wonders if they can really forget the violence that came before. Is purification the right response? *Should* one clean away all traces of violence and just forget? And James doesn't understand why, if he's making a prayer to the rock when he picks it up, he would then throw the rock away. It seems to him that he's throwing away his prayer, turning it into nothing.

Eyal Goldberg, a Yale directing student from Israel and our assistant director for the final rehearsal period, shares his thoughts on the matter:

> In the tradition where I'm from in Jerusalem, part of cleansing is accepting the fact that the violent thing happened. So when you threw the rocks, I understood it that way—not as if the prayer was nothing. Throwing the rocks in this new manner is like showing the scar: it's still there, it doesn't disappear. You are accepting what has happened and saying it won't happen again.

James appreciates this explanation, saying, "Okay, we'll try it that way."

MOUSSA'S SOLO TEXT AND DJÉDJÉ AND NAI'S SOUND-POEM DUET

Tracie, uneasy with the extent of her contribution so far, brings in a lot of new material. She's working on a new solo text for Moussa and a duet for Djédjé and Nai, both of which will introduce a more specific reference to the transatlantic slave trade and the African diaspora. She writes for Moussa in English: a simple story about going to buy toys for his daughters, getting hit on the head, losing consciousness and waking up in a completely different world. It isn't set in a specific place or time, but the resonances should be clear. For Djédjé and Nai she's just begun working on a sound-poem duet, which will incorporate short syllables and phrases in

French, English and Bete. She imagines their duet as a terse dialogue between two African chiefs-turned-slaves, calling to each other as they lie chained in the bottom of a slave ship, making the perilous Middle Passage. Tracie also brings in pages of old haikus, from which Ralph selects several that intrigue him and asks her to write more in the same vein.

The aesthetic differences between Ralph and Tracie become increasingly apparent. Tracie wants her text to provide a specific context and references, while Ralph is concerned not to be "too literal" or "too blatant." His context is the history and present reality of the African diaspora, but he doesn't want to make a didactic work *about* that subject—and he seems secretly afraid that that's what Tracie would prefer. If she brings in five poems for perusal, Ralph is sure to pick the one that's most abstract. As a result we keep on working with material that has a very specific purpose and subtext for Tracie but will never be able to convey as specific a reference for the audience. There's a discrepancy between what Tracie hopes to attain with her words and what her words are actually doing.

Aesthetic differences are also apparent in the work on the "Overview" poem. Carlos and Ralph have been trying since the beginning to find and maintain a strong relationship in their performance of the poem, but the goal proves elusive. Some rehearsals it's there, others it disappears. Tracie offers to explain the meanings behind the more obscure parts of the dialogue, but Ralph usually refuses, saying that he'd prefer the poem to remain mysterious. Peter, Tracie and I spend a lot of time trying to convince Ralph that, in this instance at least, his love of multiple meanings has gone too far, that he must choose a specific connection to the words, as a performer, if the audience is to be able to hear those words at all.

We hold frequent informal showings. I watch from far back in the house and realize with dismay that the proscenium and the cavernous onstage space are swallowing up a good deal of the performers' energy. Unfortunately I've done most of my observing until now standing onstage with the dancers or sitting in the first few rows of the house. Now it doesn't seem right, by comparison, to have the performers so distant, and enclosed by such a formal visual frame. What's more, the sound seems muffled—without scenery to bounce it out to the audience, it's floating up into the flies instead. Ralph tells the performers that they must readjust their energy to the large space, since they're no longer performing in the small spaces of upstate New York and Brooklyn. The proscenium effect is unavoidable, but we'll need to search for some concrete solutions to the sound problem. Perhaps some sort of sonic baffle could be placed up in the flies? Perhaps Nari's drum treatments (he's wrapped the *djembes* in the fabric from mattress covers) need to be removed? Experiments will follow.

Injuries and exhaustion threaten the company, but we avoid any major catastrophes, and the work presses on. James is often seen with a bag of frozen peas, using them to ice his knee or his hip. The biggest scare comes from Moussa, who hears a snapping sound in his knee late one night as he rehearses a difficult step one time too many. He's in great pain and can't walk. Carla Jackson (company manager) takes him to the emergency room, where he receives a leg brace, crutches, ice and medication and is told to stay off it for at least a week. According to Orida, Moussa then went home and immediately took off the brace, threw it and the crutches into a closet and shut the door firmly. Moussa told her that if he became accustomed to a brace and crutches, he'd never get well. He doesn't trust Western medicine. Instead he uses his own techniques, staying home for two days and meditating on his knee. When he returns to rehearsal, he starts in with the dance, exactly as before. Ralph and I wonder if we should stop him, but he assures us he is the best judge of his limits.

September 30–October 13

There's a scramble to resolve glaring technical questions. Will the ceiling fan fold up and rise into the flies for the Divination section, or will it come down and be disassembled by the dancers on stage? Will the reversible jacket being built for Goulei (blood-red on the inside; he reverses it at the close of the Rock Throwing section) need to be duplicated for other dancers as well?

We listen to the drums both with and without Nari's drum covers, standing far out in the house. Consensus is that the drum covers mute the sound very slightly, but the real problem is the sound going up into the flies. We'll keep the covers on then, since

Charles Funn, Goulei Tchépoho, Zaoli Mabo Tapé and Djeli Moussa Diabaté. Photograph by T. Charles Erickson.

the difference is small. But a solution to the flies problem isn't looking hopeful. We may have to accept the situation as is. The burden falls to Tapé and Goulei, who say they'll play as loudly as they can.

The tech crew experiments endlessly with the raising of the bottle curtains. The back curtain will fly down, but the legs on the sides will rise up, as imagined, from the floor. That is, if all the kinks can be worked out of the system. The rising bottles tend to get tangled in their supporting cables. First a solution appears to be found: if plastic ties attach the cables at the bottom as well as the top of each bottle, the wires are drawn tauter and the tangling potential is much reduced. But then the problem continues: if the bottles are left piled for a while before they need to fly, as they inevitably will be during a show, settling occurs and they tangle as before. The latest solution is sheets of black fabric laid in between each row of bottles. The unfortunate consequence of this solution is that the piles no longer look like innocuous heaps of glass but rather like something more theatrical.

Almost all the costumes are finished. I am surprised one morning to find that the performance suits are not in dark business colors, like the rehearsal suits had been, but rather in light shades of linen cloth—tan, mint green, sky blue, pale yellow. Apparently I missed it when, back in August, Liz Prince and Ralph discussed the somber palette of the set and decided that the suits needed to contrast with their environment.

During the Divination section, the entire company will wear gowns and thus be transformed into the ancestor/spirit mode. Now that we have the finished costumes, we find difficulties with skirts as tripping hazards. The dancers adjust the choreography so that they can hold their skirts in one hand most of the time. Ralph also begins rehearsing the Divination Dance to DJ Spooky's new contribution, a gripping, unnerving piece of music that sounds like it's been collaged together from the tense bits of thriller-movie soundtracks.

ENDURANCE

Ralph decides to end Divination with two dancers incessantly repeating the same few steps, over and over and over. When he first tells me of this idea, I laugh. It's the choreographic return of the repressed, I tell him. For months you've been telling them not to repeat, and now you want to let it all back in, with a vengeance. He agrees, saying that he's been interested in how his body refuses to repeat versus how their bodies seem to crave repetition. Perhaps they are just two different methods of reaching a similar goal of transcendence.

Ralph chooses a new musical track by Francisco that crescendos slowly to an ear-splitting din and then breaks off suddenly into silence. The selection takes about seven minutes to complete, and the dance that will accompany it earns, for obvious reasons, the label Endurance (with a French accent, no matter who is speaking). Djédjé and James take on the task of performing it. Each puts together a repetitive loop of three or four demanding African steps and tries to enter a "zone" that will enable him to dance all the way through without flagging. Ralph asks Angelo and Nai to enter and accompany Djédjé and James for selected measures as their "energy-boosters." But for the most part the two are alone on stage. Like marathoners reaching the home stretch, their movement gets faster, fuller and more exquisite the closer they get to the end. Just before the peak of the crescendo James dances off stage and leaves Djédjé alone to finish the final moments—when the sound cuts out, he's usually in midair, dreadlocks flying, and requires a few seconds to decelerate. Then he turns in place twice and simply walks off the stage.

This is as close as Ralph gets to the Meditation Dance he could never figure out how to stage—a passage of choreography that appeals less for its formal beauty and more for the internal state that it requires of the dancer. Peter is amazed and finds it incredibly moving. I agree, but my immediate focus is on the performers' welfare: can they really do this every night, after a whole show's worth of dancing? We sit down to discuss the situation. Djédjé tells us that he's a professional and he's danced equally hard at home before. It is difficult, true; but if Ralph thinks it's good for the show, they'll do it. James agrees. With that green light Ralph continues shaping the Endurance section, especially the timing of Angelo and Nai's entrances and exits.

October 14

Today is our first run-through of the entire show. Joining us in the audience are Stan Wojewodski, Jr. and Mark Bly (associate artistic director of the Yale Rep), both eager to see where we are now. I am charged with taking detailed notes on the performers' execution as Ralph will, for all run-throughs hereafter, remain on stage as part of the company.

Afterward we discuss many issues, but the most heated discussion crops up around the text. Tracie broaches the subject with a slight edge in her voice:

> Tonight I'm trying to figure out what purpose the text is serving. It's becoming pure composition, and it's losing the grounding purpose we'd talked about before. If that's supposed to be the case, okay; but let's be clear about it. But if it should be grounding us, then we need to work on it. At this point the dancers' spontaneous vocal expressions—when they yell to encourage each other during Collage, or when they make rhythms vocally—are grounding this piece in a way the text is not. We need to figure this out.

Akpa Yves Didier ("James," far left), Djeli Moussa Diabaté (on ladder) and Ralph Lemon (far right). Photograph by T. Charles Erickson.

Ralph responds that we have to be honest about how grounding poetry really can be, especially when he's selected the most abstract passages. He's always thought of the text as music more than anything else. Stan breaks in and asks Tracie what she would want to have happen, in order to make the text more grounding. She replies that certain things that are not here now would have to be introduced—like the duet for Djédjé and Nai about the Middle Passage. Also, Ralph and Carlos need to work on really speaking to each other during the "Overview" poem; the relationship doesn't seem real. But she needs to know why this text is here.

Mark interjects and tells us that he came away this evening wondering what the piece would be like with no text at all. He doesn't mean that it should be scrapped—it's too early for that. But he simply did not find the support for it. There were no signposts for it, no moments that said, Listen to this.

This is the most helpful explanation I've heard so far, and yet, unfortunately, I find it discouraging, because I've no idea how to help Ralph find those signposts. His approach is so nonlinear that concepts such as "signposts" haven't been part of our vocabulary. Ralph sighs and says, "That's the question. This is an absolutely nonlinear event, that's a given, but words have other expectations attached. . . ." We end the meeting at a low point. The text problems are clearer, but the clarity is sobering.

October 15-27: Technical rehearsals and previews

With Ralph up on stage I am drawn further into the details. My notes are increasingly full of corrections for the performers ("Angelo and Djédjé, stay together when hand goes over head. . . . Carlos, more attack on Collage. . . . Djédjé and James, when starting Endurance, don't telegraph the fact you'll be dancing forever. . . ."). The evolving routine is that I give these notes to Ralph every night, and he writes down some of them to process himself and asks me to give others directly to the performers.

And now, as we enter the tedious slow rhythms of tech, I'm often occupied as a second interpreter. I'm sure I've done my part to gravitate toward this increasingly involved role—I certainly didn't resist it. I am, however, losing my clear view of the larger picture.

DJÉDJÉ AND NAI'S DUET: "MENE MENE"

We incorporate Tracie's duet for Djédjé and Nai into the piece. The poem is called "Mene Mene," after the first two words of the "Overview" poem as translated, by Djédjé, into the Bete language. Djédjé and Nai call to each other across the stage, trading short phrases with punning relationships: "Mene Mene" becomes "many Benin." "Très chaud" becomes "sho' nuf," which becomes "show." Tracie has discussed the context of the poem thoroughly with Djédjé and Nai, and as a result their delivery is strong and somber. Ralph first tries "Mene Mene" at the very end of the show, then moves it earlier into the Crime section, placing Moussa's Solo Text at the end. He discovers a way to overlap "Mene Mene" with Carlos and James's Path Phrase Duet, and this opens up a whole new world. Suddenly the text is integrated in a way it has never quite been before. Up until now there was either dancing or talking, but never both at once.

Come previews, we have a show to present, but it is not a finished product. Notes continue full force, and rehearsals are held every day. Transitions between scenes have suffered neglect and are only just beginning to be finessed. And the Divination Dance still needs attention.

Ralph continues to experiment with new ideas in front of an audience. Part of his hard look at what it means to be a black

dancer on the stage is a hard look at the tradition of black entertainment. From the beginning he told the Africans about the long
history of African-American entertainers who, trying to make it
in a hostile environment, survived by marketing their culture as
entertainment for the white world. Now he tries different ways to
make this theme more explicit. He doesn't always warn me, and so
one night I am surprised, in the middle of "Overview," to see a
bright spotlight pop up center stage and Ralph walking into it,
cooing the opening of a Temptations song into his mike. Then, just
as abruptly, he stops and resumes his dialogue with Carlos. It's no
accident that questions of why and for whom the performance occurs
have surfaced at this time, now that we have a formal audience.

October 28–November 8: Opening night and beyond

Audience reactions are widely, widely varied. Some people adore
the show with a fervor bordering on devotion—one friend of mine
visiting from New York extends his stay just so he can see the performance a second time. My undergraduate theatre students beg
me for extra tickets. Other audience members can't understand
what they are being asked to watch. Unprepared for Ralph's brand
of abstraction, they leave the auditorium in an uneasy haze.
Certain others dislike the show for more precisely articulated reasons, some of which I can respect and others not. I speak to one
older white woman who is angry because Ralph has taken African
dancing, a form that is so quintessentially entertaining, and *refused*
to entertain her with it! I can't help but think of Ralph's statements
on black entertainers throughout American history and conclude
that this is exactly the reaction Ralph would want from this particular audience member. Another woman, a black teacher of
dance and drama at a local high school, orders a large block of tickets for her students but then refuses to bring them after seeing the

show herself two nights earlier. She also refuses to return the tickets to the box office, leaving a gaping hole in the audience that night. She tells the marketing office that she can't allow her kids to see such a negative view of African men. I never find out more specifically what she was reacting to—the fact that they wore gowns? the violence of the rock throwing? the overall feeling of dislocation and exile?

I think the source of all this disparity is in the fact that *Geography* served as something of a Rorschach ink blot on the themes of the African diaspora. What the viewer saw depended, to an extraordinary degree, on his or her personal relation to those themes. As Ralph intended, *Geography* posed questions instead of offering clear statements, and offered little in the way of linear progression. Even during the final Divination section, with all the many glass bottles suspended like dewdrops on a spider web, any feelings of transcendence could easily be counterbalanced by the anxious tones of DJ Spooky's music or the profound dislocation described in Moussa's final text. There were many different moods and ideas conveyed, but no one catagorizable statement. Some found it mysteriously evocative, some found it mystifying. My primary role during Yale's postshow discussions was to assure the audience that there was no one single secret "right answer" to the images they had experienced.

At the most basic level *Geography* told two reciprocal stories. One was the story of the company's actual collaboration—the struggle to find new ways to dance together, with triumphant, intriguing results. The other was the story of the unbridgeable distances that separated the company members and the echoes of the diaspora and colonialism that still haunt the world today. When Ralph broke down African dance forms into component parts, it was both a taking apart as a source for new, creative, recombinations and a taking apart to indicate a theme of emotional fragmentation. Ralph was not interested in telling one story at the expense of the other. The answer to any inquiry on this matter was always, "Both."

Of course, the one story that Ralph *wasn't* telling, at least not in any literal sense, was *The Oresteia*. The pursuit of that narrative had petered out long ago. As diligent dramaturgs, Peter and I were the last to give up the chase, but even we had realized, way back in midsummer, that our responsibility was to the work as it was evolving, not as it had been articulated in advance. The plot and characters of *The Oresteia* had served their purpose as scaffolding, falling away as soon as the work could stand on its own. But *The Oresteia's* deeper imagery—the powerfully resonant themes of intra-familial violence, exile, and justice—had always remained at the core of Ralph's investigations.

I watched the show for several days past opening night before I stopped going to the theatre, out of complete exhaustion. The last night in New Haven an enormous truck pulled up next to the University Theatre, ready to pack up all the materials for the tour. I didn't see the show again, or the company, until December, when I went to a performance at BAM's Majestic Theater. The bottles no longer rose into the air—too many disasters over the touring period, so now all the curtains came down from the flies while Goulei imitated the clinking sound of bottles going up, sitting atop a ladder with two bottles and a stick. But over the tour Ralph had continued to make changes and had worked all the transitions until they were smoother, more fully formed, less utilitarian. The show had a real breath to it. Audiences were warm and better conditioned for Ralph's nonlinear approach than the audiences in New Haven. The New York press was largely positive.

I feel that I finally *saw* the finished show, sitting there as an anonymous audience member in the Majestic. I was a little sad during certain textual sections, thinking that we'd still never found enough places for Tracie's words to flourish within the onstage world. But watching Collage/Quartet or Minuet or Rock Throwing or Divination, I felt the same shivers of amazement that I had from the first. I was watching a kind of dancing that was new to everyone dancing it, both African and American. The performers transmitted that sense of discovery, subtly but undeniably, in every move they made.

Katherine Profeta worked as a dramaturg for Julie Taymor on such projects as Fool's Fire, Oedipus Rex, Titus Andronicus *and* The Green Bird *before entering the Yale School of Drama's Dramaturgy and Dramatic Criticism program. As a student, she worked with Ralph Lemon on* Geography. *After receiving her MFA, she continued her work with Lemon on* The Geography Trilogy: *part 2, entitled* Tree, *a collaboration with Asian artists, premiered at the Yale Rep in the spring of 2000 before moving to BAM and other venues; part 3, entitled* House *a collaboration with artists from the southern United States, is currently in preparation. Katherine is also a founding member and choreographer for Elevator Repair Service, a New York experimental theatre group, and a freelance dramaturg for Theatre for a New Audience. She presently teaches movement and dramatic literature at Barnard College.*

SELECT BIBLIOGRAPHY

Aeschylus. *The Oresteia*. Translated by David Grene and Wendy Doniger O'Flaherty. Chicago: The University of Chicago Press, 1989.

Fanon, Frantz. *Black Skin, White Masks*. Translated by Charles Lam Markmann. New York: Grove Press, 1987.

Somé, Malidoma Patrice. *Of Water and the Spirit: Ritual, Magic and Initiation in the Life of an African Shaman*. New York: Putnam, 1994.

Vogel, Susan Mullin. *Baule: African Art, Western Eyes*. New Haven, CT: Yale University Press in cooperation with the Museum for African Art, 1997.